The Big Horse

The Big Horse AND OTHER
STORIES OF MODERN MACEDONIA

Edited, with an introduction by
Milne Holton

University of Missouri Press
Columbia 1974

ISBN 0–8262–0162–8
Copyright © 1974 by
The Curators of the University of Missouri
Library of Congress Catalog Card Number 73–93892
Printed and bound in the United States of America
University of Missouri Press, Columbia, Missouri 65201

For My Mother

Acknowledgments

I wish to acknowledge the valued advice and continuing assistance of Graham and Margaret Reid and Ivanka Koviloska-Poposka of the University of Skopje and the steady encouragement of Bogomil Gjuzel and Dr. Gane Todorovski. The Federal Ministry of Information in Belgrade has provided valuable advice and assistance, and the Fulbright Commission has generously supported my work.

Peter Boškovski of Skopje has recently completed a collection of Macedonian short stories for publication in their original language. His collection has served as a source for my own. However, the final responsibility for the choice of stories is entirely mine.

Last, I would thank Meto Jovanovski, the inspiration and guiding force behind this collection. Without his steady encouragement and unstinting support and assistance, the completion of this work would not have been possible.

M. H.
College Park, Maryland
February, 1974

A Note on the Translations

The translations were prepared from literal renderings of the stories into English by Mr. Alan McConnell. Editorial changes have been restricted to those instances in which a strictly literal translation altered meaning as it would be received in the original language.

Brief Guide to the Pronunciation of Macedonian Names

Although the Macedonian language is written in the Cyrillic alphabet, proper names are set here in the Latin alphabet and are spelled as they would be in Croatian. Like Serbian, Croatian is basically spelled as it is pronounced, one symbol representing one sound. But sometimes letters are used two or three times, with differing diacritical marks to indicate that they are being used for differing sounds. Most letters have sounds equivalent to their sound in English. Set forth below are approximate sounds for other letters.

c - ts
ć - tsh
č - ch
g - hard, as in English "go"
j - y (consonant)
š - sh
ž - zh
dz - soft, as in "George"
gj - same as *dz*, except slightly more voiced, as the *j* in English "jar"
h - ch as in "Bach"

Generally, Macedonian is distinguished from the other Yugoslav languages in its permanent accent on the antepenultimate (third from last) syllable. In two-syllable names, the accent falls on the first syllable.

Contents

Brief Guide to the Pronunciation of Macedonian Names, vi

Introduction, 1

Simon Drakul, *The Big Horse*, 7

Meto Jovanovski, *The Man in the Blue Suit*, 18

Vlado Maleski, *Dipithon*, 25

Kole Čašule, *A Macedonian Girl*, 43

Cvetko Martinovski, *Early Evening*, 57

Živko Čingo, *Argil's Decoration*, 71

Dimitar Solev, *The Round Trip of a Shadow*, 79

Mile Nedelkovski, *The Body That Belonged to No One*, 92

Blaže Koneski, *The Final Move*, 97

Jovan Boškovski, *The Man on the Roof*, 107

Petre M. Andreevski, *The Vampire*, 113

Taško Georgievski, *The Women on the Little Wooden Stools*, 120

Meto Fotev, *The Witness*, 126

Srbo Ivanovski, *The Shirt*, 141

Božin Pavlovski, *Border Incident*, 146

Bogomil Gjuzel, *The Typewriter*, 161

Branko Varošlija, *The Strong, Hot Wind*, 172

Olivera Nikolova, *Saturday Evening*, 183

Vlada Urošević, *The Tailor's Dummy*, 191

Vladimir Kostov, *The Game*, 198

Introduction

The name *Macedonia* is for many rich in suggestion but difficult to specify. One remembers vaguely from one's schooldays the facts surrounding Alexander the Great's origins—the son of Philip who was "of Macedon," somewhere to the north of Greece. This young prince had come to Athens and had studied under Aristotle before conquering the world. But this memory helps us very little, for Alexander's empire, which may well have had its beginnings elsewhere, had collapsed long before the coming of the Slav peoples to the valley of the Vardar River, which empties into the Aegean at the city now called Salonika, and before they had settled in on its rich plains and in the mountains rising from them, on the east where there is now the Bulgarian border and on the west where there is presently Albania. The Slavs did not come to this Macedonia until the sixth century, and Alexander's name is given little attention there today. Although the population of Macedonia has for hundreds of years been a mixture of many different ethnic groups—Greeks, Albanians, Vlachs, Gypsies, Turks—Macedonian culture has been predominately Slav since the sixth century.

To the Latinist, Macedonia is also rich in associations; the Via Ignatia passed through the area, and there were important Roman settlements at Heracleum near Bitola and at Stobi, near Veles. But again, it is not Roman culture that is important; Macedonia is orthodox in tradition and therefore shows Byzantine influence. And to the Byzantinist the area is rich in association indeed.

In Salonika in the ninth century it was an Orthodox monk, Cyril, who composed an alphabet for the language of the Slavs. The Macedonian churches—Sv. Kliment and Sv. Sophia at Ohrid, Sv. Naum across the lake to the south,

Sv. Pantalimon at Nerezi, near Skopje, Sv. Jovan Bigorski on Lake Mavrovo, and many others—are clear evidence of the Byzantine influence. Their frescoes and their architecture are almost all that remains of the glory and profundity of medieval Macedonia. Stefan Dušan, the greatest of the Nemanjan monarchs, was crowned at Skopje in 1346, and for a time he made Markovgrad (on a mountain near Prilep) the capital of his brilliant empire. But that empire was to last for only forty more years before its glory was extinguished at Kosovo on the Plain of the Blackbirds where, in 1389, Tzar Lazar's army was smashed by the Turks.

The student of the Renaissance, the Reformation, the Enlightenment will know little of Macedonia, for there was no Renaissance, no Enlightenment in that land. For the next four hundred years Macedonia was a conquered territory under Turkish oppression, and its principal cultural struggle was a struggle for preservation and for the vitalization of the memory of past times. Church Slavonic was turned increasingly to otherworldly purposes; the only secular works of the imagination known today are the dark epic poems of the Battle of Kosovo. There are also songs about Kralje Marko, the legendary despot who has become a figure of heroic legend in his struggles against the Sultan, who absorbed the images of the Thracian horseman, St. George, and even of Stefan Dušan himself.

For the modern historian, however, the name *Macedonia* is well known but pitiable. Macedonia was stirred to concerted struggle against her oppressors by the success of the Serbian Revolution in 1815; her struggles soon became the concern of the new Serbian state, and of Bulgaria, and of the Western nations. Gladstone excited the sympathies of Englishmen in 1897 with his plea for "Macedonia for the Macedonians," and soon Macedonia came to be known as the site of the last great struggle for ethnic self-realization. It also came to be known as the land of outrages and of *comitadji* reprisal, of IMRO and VMRI. And in 1903, in the Ilinden uprising, Macedonian revolutionaries even proclaimed a republic, which lasted for eleven days.

But as Turkish domination receded and under Atatürk (who had been educated at Bitola) was finally withdrawn, Macedonia found her new masters—Serbia and Bulgaria—competing for control. During the First World War her land provided a critical battleground, Kajmakčalan near Bitola, the mountain stormed by Serbian and French troops whose victory made possible the Serbian army's triumphant return to Belgrade in 1916. But after that war (and another in the Balkans) Macedonia was simply partitioned—among Bulgaria, Greece, and the new Yugoslav kingdom.

So it was not until after the Second World War and the successful struggle of Tito's partisans and the forging of a new Yugoslavia that Macedonia realized in some measure her autonomy as a republic, federated within that new state. It was only then that she had her own university, that Macedonian became the teaching language of her schools, and that she achieved a variety of self-government. It is pride in these achievements that has shaped the consciousness of her people.

That consciousness has been articulated—especially since the Second World War—in a literature written in a language that is at once the oldest and the newest of the Slavic tongues. There is good evidence to suggest that the alphabet formed by Cyril at Ohrid in the ninth century—the alphabet of Old Slavonic, which was to form the basis for what is now known as Cyrillic script—was in fact a transcription of the sounds of the language of the Macedonian Slavs. Whether or not this may be true, it is certain that the Macedonian language in its modern form had only the most meager of beginnings as a literary language until well into the second half of the nineteenth century. Then there were efforts to establish Macedonian as a language for poetry—by such men as Grigor Prličev and by the Miladinov brothers at Ohrid and Struga. And there were rather more vigorous efforts to replace Greek with Macedonian as the language of churches and schools. After the First World War, however, when Macedonia was partitioned, Macedonian became a forbidden language; it is still so in Greece—from the dictatorship of Metaxas to the present.

In the 1930s Macedonia began to reemerge as a literary language, first (and most easily) in the drama, later as a language of songs and newspapers. In 1939 Kočo Račin (who was later to become a partisan martyr) published a first collection of poems, *Beli Mugri* (*The Dawn*), in Zagreb. But there was really no literary movement, and no prose fiction worthy of the name, until after the Liberation in 1945. Thus it was only after the war, when Blaže Koneski, then a young scholar at the University of Skopje, formulated an alphabet and an orthography for the language, that modern Macedonian as a literary language could really be said to have been established.

So what we have before us is a collection of stories translated from a literary language that is in a sense only slightly more than a quarter of a century old. Yet, in that quarter century the development has been a truly astounding one, and that development is perhaps most dramatically apparent in the short story. As one might imagine, in the years immediately following the war in which the new Yugoslav Federal Republic was still heavily under the influence of Soviet policy—in matters intellectual as well as economic—the short stories of the Macedonians had their beginning in social realism. But even the early stories were affected by a strong flavor of regional lyricism, a strain that has remained vigorous in more recent stories.

After Tito's break with Stalin in 1948, Party control of literature in Yugoslavia gradually relaxed, interference became the exception rather than the rule, and, more important, the act of creative expression came to be separated in the minds of intellectuals as well as of politicians from the political act. By the early or middle fifties Macedonian writers had for the most part turned away from the tradition of social realism to a deeper commitment to a regional tradition. This tradition has lain deep in the Macedonian consciousness, and with the emergence of a literature it took a particularly lyric form, strengthened no doubt by the long years of frustration of ethnic self-realization and by longing for the homeland known to her many emigrés. Generations of Macedonians for hundreds of years had been forced to leave their villages to wander the world in search of the employment that was unavailable at home. Sooner or later many of them returned to their native soil, but others remained in lifelong exile.

Since the late 1950s, the young writers coming out of the universities, sometimes after a period of study abroad, have been looking in new directions and are exploring new interests. Liberalization of control of the press has now developed to a point at which there is no reason to believe that a Macedonian writer today is significantly less free to express himself and to publish his work than his counterpart in western Europe or in America. With these developments the impulse of Macedonian writers of the short story, both formally and in their choices of subject matter, has been increasingly outward, first toward imitation and then toward creative participation in the developing mainstream of European writing. Despite the expansion of their horizons, these present-day Macedonian writers have never forgotten their native region, its beauty, and its traditions.

There have been at least two generations of writers in Macedonia since the war. The younger of the two—the writers who were too young to have been partisans—has produced far more stories worthy of note than the elder, and, because of their new freedom and new awareness, their stories are increasingly disparate. They demonstrate new influences as well (of Ionesco upon Urošević, for example). They recognize new possibilities for the representation of fantasy-experience in their fiction, and they explore these possibilities with the new forms and narrative procedures made available by the work of the antistory modernists.

Even in their awareness of these new developments, however, it is possible to recognize in these younger writers'
works the impact of more distinctly Macedonian influences;
the influence of the older postwar writers is not lost on the
younger generation. The old lyric regionalism is still there,
albeit in a more anguished state, as these new writers explore the new patterns of human relationships for a village
people only recently come to the city. The old sense of place
and the old pride in the beauty of place is there, although
sometimes only in a sense of loss, in a keen awareness of the
essential negativeness of modern urban places. And, even
for this new generation of writers, there is still an apparent
delight in the new possibilities of expression in a language
that is new and fresh and that is still very much their own.

*   *   *   *

In choosing the stories to be included in this collection, I
have made no attempt to include representative examples of
the work of all Macedonian writers who are held in high
regard by their countrymen. Several of Macedonia's most
distinguished and best-known writers of fiction—Slavko
Janevski, Blagoja Ivanov, Petar Širilov, and Branko Pen-
dovski among them—have not been represented here. In
choosing stories for inclusion, I have been guided more by
a desire to represent as selectively as possible something
of the range of matter and manner in Macedonian fiction
today than by the impulse to anthologize her best-known
and most widely acclaimed writers of short stories. So,
while I hope that my collection can be regarded as representative in the narrow sense here described, I make no claim
for its comprehensiveness.

The Big Horse

"What's that! An earthquake?"

"Look! Look!"

Then they fell silent. I was lying under a blanket, but I could hear the rattling of gunfire, and all the windowpanes began to shiver, as though somebody was shaking our whole house.

"My God, but it's close! You'd think they were just behind the house," said my mother.

"Heavens, what a noise," whispered Granny.

Then the windows rattled again. The cat was beside me. Every now and then it drew in its claws and stroked me with the soft pads of its paws. Mischievously. But what was making the windows rattle so? And why had Mother and Granny gotten up so early? And what was this deep booming, so powerful that it seemed to be coming from somewhere close behind us? My mother asked the same question —what could this noise be?

Simon Drakul was born in 1930 in Lazarpole. In 1940 Drakul, then ten years old, fled to Ohrid, where he completed his schooling, and, after the Liberation, he settled in Skopje where he studied at the Faculty of Philosophy and worked first as a teacher and then as a journalist. He has served as the Director of Drama at the Macedonian National Theatre in Skopje and has recently completed his tenure of office as Secretary of the Macedonian Writers' Union.

Drakul is known today primarily as a fictionist and translator, although he began his career as a poet and has written for the theatre and the film. His first collection of stories, *The Mountain and the Distances*, appeared in 1953, and another collection, *Whirlpools in the Flood*, was published in 1956. There have since been two novels, *The Stars Fall on Their Own* (1957) and the remarkable *The White Valley* (1962).

Earthquakes, as well as wars, are not uncommon in Macedonia. Skopje was virtually destroyed by an earthquake in 1963.

Now I can see them. They were sitting behind the fire, but they were not holding the spindles they usually had in their hands. They were sunk in thought. The ruddy, flickering light from the log burning in the fireplace mingled with the unsteady glow of the lamp in front of the icon.

"Like an earthquake—those hellish cannons," said Mother.

Cannons! How could that be? Cannons? Were those real cannons rumbling so relentlessly somewhere far away and yet close by? Was it really cannon fire that was making the windows rattle? How could that be? Cannons? But something had to be making the noise. They must have been cannons after all. And since they were cannons . . .

"Why are you sitting up in bed like a frightened hedgehog?" somebody shouted at me. Granny was shouting at me and glaring angrily. She had to vent her anger on somebody. That somebody was me. I sat up in bed, came out from under the blanket. There I was—uncovered. But that face, which had always been kindly, softened now and recovered its usual expression: soft, velvety, and yet thoughtful and somewhat unpleasantly ruddy, reddened by the glow of the burning log.

"What's that noise, Granny?" I asked. The soft, ruddy face did not look at me. Granny was again hunched up in front of the fire. They were staring at the embers. The windows rattled again. This time we were shaken more violently. Granny and Mother glanced at each other. Then they stared at the embers. At first I waited for them to give me an answer, but then I began listening to the deep rumbles rolling on, one after another, like underground thunder— the booming of what must have been cannons somewhere in the distance, in the night. I listened to the windows rattling, and I watched the glass panes reddening with the dawn. I may have even asked once again what the noise was, but they did not answer. I too stared at the embers.

I got my answer the next day, which dawned with the

reddening sunrise. It was an almost autumnal day early in spring. How many yesterdays since had I seen a swallow sweeping low down over the school yard? And yet it was still an autumnal day, gray and murky. Only occasionally would light spill out over the broad sweep of the hills, but it was like the glow of a distant fire. Then the grayness would seem even worse, more oppressive, as though the sky had been sprinkled with ashes. The deep booming was carried even more clearly by the wind to us from a faraway place behind the hills. The wind kept bringing the sound, and the windows seemed never to stop rattling—in all the houses of the village. Then, when the grayness of the afternoon began to darken and turn murky with the dusk that was blowing over the hills, the first soldiers began to pass along the outskirts of the village. They did not have guns. Their greatcoats were discolored and dirty from the red dust, like the departing day. They carried blankets rolled up like doughnuts over their shoulders. Their faces were tired. They had come from far away. Their skin was raw and red, dried out by the wind. In many other ways as well they resembled the day that had just passed, perhaps because they too had stolen in over the hills, slipped past the houses on the edge of the village, and then gone off, silently, muffled in their greatcoats. The day also seemed to have stolen away. But even so, that day had told me that somewhere, on the border, war had begun. This war was rolling along the roads somewhere, and down the valleys. This was what made the windows rattle.

Then more soldiers passed. They were dog-tired. Several of them were not carrying blankets rolled up like doughnuts. These would slink past in groups, quiet, dirty, silent. People said that they were running away.

The next morning the windows rattled again. In the distance the booming of the cannons reverberated like underground thunder. War was rolling along the valleys. The daylight was again gray, wind-streaked, like the soldiers' greatcoats. And the river, like the drifting flush of the sun spattered on the hills, was the same dusty red as the soldiers' greatcoats.

And so the days stole past. One, two, three . . .

Each morning the windows rattled, and the cat pawed. But the lamp in front of the icon continued to burn. Granny and Mother stared thoughtfully at the live coals in the fireplace.

"Like an earthquake," whispered Granny.

"You'd think it was right behind the house, it's so close," said Mother.

Mother had been rather silent that morning, but finally she whispered, "Where can he be now? Many of them have already arrived, but he still hasn't come." She was thinking of Father. We had been expecting him every day, and now every moment. He was somewhere out there where the cannons were rumbling. He would be wearing a dirty greatcoat, like all the soldiers who were passing. But although they kept on coming right through the night, Father still was not among them. How could it be that he still had not come when so many had already come?

"Heavens, what a noise!" whispered Granny. Again the windows rattled. The cannons were roaring more and more frequently now. The noise oppressed us. There was booming on the border, where Father was. And now the ashy whiteness of dawn was spilling through the windowpanes.

"Soon he will come back," Granny went on. She did not want us to keep silent. The silence and the expectation had wound us up to a breaking point. The tension was so great that it even seemed to be spluttering out of the log in the fireplace. Perhaps that was why Granny stood up. Or perhaps the strain of waiting made it impossible for her to remain seated. She walked over to the window, then stood there, gazing out. She had probably been deceived by a reflection that had seemed to her like a soldier's face, tired, weatherbeaten, covered with a long dirty beard and smiling at her—or so I imagined my father's face in those days of waiting.

"Come here and look," said Granny.

It was then I saw it—the big horse. It was coming out of the alley across the road; it was black, enormous. I had never seen such a huge horse. One could have made out of him several little horses the size of the other one to which it was attached by a halter. The big horse's steps were slow, steady, heavy, while the little horse in front of him seemed to be almost running to stay ahead. It was gray, like a mouse, and somebody was riding it. The big animal seemed to be heavily loaded. It was carrying on either side something dark and shiny, and as it moved the load swung rhythmically. But who could this rider be?

"Wo-ooah!" As soon as I heard this I knew it was our neighbor, Dojčin. And the little pony was Čilko. Čilko really was a tiny animal, but I had not realized until then that he was quite so small. Čilko stopped in front of the gate of Dojčin's house. The big horse stopped, and the pony nuzzled his own flank. Old Dojčin dismounted hurriedly and led Čilko up to the gate. Čilko resisted. Then he moved forward, taking tiny steps. But suddenly he stopped. The big horse seemed to be fixed firmly in the alley. He did not so much as move his head.

"Move, you brute!" shouted Dojčin.

Čilko started to move again. Or, more exactly, he stamped in the alley without taking a single step forward. His hoofs struck bright sparks from the cobblestones. The big horse now lifted his head a little but still made no movement forward.

"M-oo-ove!" shouted the old man.

Čilko's hoofs struck a few more sparks. Then he seemed almost propelled into the yard. Inside, next to the gate, old Dojčin was lying on the ground groaning. The big horse was still standing in the alley, as if rooted to the spot. The end of his halter was now attached only to Čilko's saddle, which was now in the dust at the gate.

"That gave him something to think about," whispered Granny. I wanted to burst out laughing.

Then old Dojčin stood up. "Sonofabitch! sonofabitch!" he shouted. Then he groaned. Then slowly, as though he had been soundly beaten, he walked up to the magnificent horse, who was standing, firm as a rock, in the alley. Dojčin seemed to be afraid of it.

"Sonofabitch! sonofabitch!" he cursed, as he untied the end of the big horse's halter from the saddle. "Sonofabitch! sonofabitch!" he cursed, as he unloaded the dark bags from the big horse's flanks. It took him several trips to carry the loads into the yard. He swore while he untied the saddle. He cursed while he loosened the halter. And as he closed the gate he cursed again for good measure. "M-oo-ove, you brute! Sonofabitch! sonofabitch!" he shouted, making ridiculous threatening gestures meant to frighten the quiet horse. Then he withdrew. The horse remained rooted to the spot. After a while Dojčin began shouting again in the yard. "Open up, woman! Sonofabitch!"

Then everything quieted down. The horse continued to stand, still as a statue in the alley. It was a magnificent creature, silhouetted dazzlingly against the whiteness of the morning.

"Many armies have come and gone, and he's seen them all off in the same way," said Granny. "He's always finding something on the road and carrying it off like this. And he always wears those leather sandals. Not long ago he was complaining to me that the sandals he got the last time the Bulgarians were here have finally worn out. He always said they wouldn't last long."

"But why did he have to bring the poor animal into the village?" said Mother. She was looking at the horse in the alley, and her eyes were full of pity. Then we heard the cannons booming again somewhere in the distance. The war was still rolling down through those distant valleys, on the border where Father was.

Later I went out into the alley, but now the big horse was gone and there was no sign of Dojčin. There were only a few curious neighborhood children.

"What enormous tracks! Look. They're like frying pans!"

"And what a strange hoof he has. You can't tell which way he went."

"But didn't you see where he went? Oh, I'd love to see him." The children peppered me with questions when we came out of the alley. I told them how old Dojčin had fallen flat on his face that morning when we first had heard the rumbling. They had a good laugh about it. "Sonofabitch! sonafabitch!" they shouted. But as we were staring awe-struck at the tracks, which really did look like frying pans, Dojčin's dirty gray face showed round the side of the gate. We scampered away.

"Sonofabitch! sonofabitch!" he yelled after us.

But when we stopped running, halfway down the hill below the alley, we came across the huge pan-shaped tracks again. We followed them, and they led us into a wide yard. Shouts were ringing out from one of the buildings, although it was unusual to hear shouting in those days. The noise seemed to be coming from the stables behind the house. A moment later we saw the big horse. Poor creature. His head was poking out through the open flap above the top of the door. Behind him, coming from the stable, one could hear shouts and the dull blows of a heavy stick being beaten against something soft. They were trying to drive him out, but he was so huge and sturdy that he could not pass through the door. He stood there calmly, as though he knew that if he could tense himself for the final effort he could find the strength to break out. If necessary he could crack a rib or two, if necessary he could break down the door, but that was what was wanted by the people who were beating him from the rear. Then he succeeded; the door gave way. He staggered out, and then ran past us through the yard and back up the hill. We had seen two sticky welts bleeding on his flanks. His cruppers were striped with the blows from

the stick. Then we listened, as the men came out and told
some bystanders what had happened.

"He went into the stable and broke the floor. Then he fell
down."

"Goddamn the brute!"

"You can't blame the horse, poor creature!"

"Poor creature, my foot!"

"It's the man who brought him into the village who's
to blame."

"I'll say! The monster knocked down my fence!"

We went in to see the enormous hole he had made in
the floor, then we stared for a long time at the shattered
door. When we came out of the yard the people had calmed
down somewhat and were murmuring.

"He'll die, poor thing!"

"They say horses like that can't graze."

We set out after him, and when we finally came upon him,
the big horse was again walking, slowly, steadily, his head
slightly lowered. We went on past him, still marveling at
every hoofprint he left. When we finally came to the top of
the hill with him, we saw a group of weary soldiers preparing to set out for somewhere. Some had stopped by
a group of women who were carrying bundles of men's
clothes, worn-out and tattered. The soldiers had stopped to
change their clothes, and now some were already dressed
as poor peasants. Long journeys lay ahead of them, and on
the way they might easily be captured. Indeed, many had
already been caught, so we heard them say.

In the afternoon when we were returning home, and
when the sunlight was again reddening the hills like the reflection of a distant fire, we saw the big horse once more.
He seemed now to be something of a stranger, standing there
alone near the top of the hill. He did not look to me as if he
felt at home. He was all on his own. A reddish glow suffused
his sleek coat and gave the impression of a strength worthy
of admiration. But how would he use his strength now, and
how would he be able to preserve it?

The cannons still rumbled, but their rumbling was quieter now, and less frequent. The windowpanes still rattled. The afternoon had changed its color from an ashen gray to an unpleasant shade of pink. The soldiers were passing. They now had all changed their clothes. The war was rolling along the roads and down the valleys. There were foreign soldiers out there now, out there from where Father was supposed to come.

When I came in the house, I saw that my mother's eyes were bloodshot from staring at the window. Granny's eyes were also fixed on the window. They were waiting, but still he had not come.

Perhaps it was because I too was tense with the waiting that I could not stay quietly at home, and the chattering of my friends in the alley again lured me outside. I ran out; my friends were watching Old Dojčin as he climbed up the hill. He was limping visibly on his right leg. He must have been hurt that morning when Čilko trampled on him. A new, yellow gun was slung over his shoulder. We set out after him. He often looked around, cursing.

"Sonofabitch! sonofabitch!"

Several groups of soldiers were still straggling up the hill. Their eyes were filled with a deep weariness. How dark their faces were now from the wind! Their beards had grown out, and they were dirty. Only a few still had greatcoats. Some were walking barefoot over the frozen ground. They hardly seemed to be able to drag themselves over to the group of women who were helping them to change their clothes and were giving them tea.

Dojčin had already crossed over the top of the hill. The soldiers were very sad, and this sadness of theirs forced me to the thought that perhaps they were the last and that still my father was not among them. But we continued to follow old Dojčin. And soon we were already climbing the next hill. He seemed to sense that we were following him. He looked round at us, but he only shouted, "Sonofabitch! sonofabitch!"

Then he was looking at something on the small trail.
There, printed clearly in the dry frost, were the horse's
huge hoofmarks. What did he want with the big horse? He
looked back again. "Sonofabitch! sonofabitch!" he cursed.
The yellow gun swung from his shoulder as he limped
along.

We found the horse up there on the next hill, behind the
thicket. He was standing dead still on the edge of the wood.
How long he had been standing there, and what he was
looking at with those clouded eyes of his, which had soaked
up the grayness of the day, no one knew. What were those
eyes dreaming of, what visions did they see? His head was
hung so low that he seemed to be bowed over something.
That vivid red sheen no longer suffused his coat. He seemed
exhausted. The welts on his flanks had dried into dark clots
of blood. His legs were covered to the knees in muck.
Dojčin had already moved up close to him. The horse glanced
at him with one eye and then stood looking at him with a
certain sadness. He looked at us.

"Sonofabitch! sonofabitch!" Dojčin cursed. He unslung
his gun, rattled the breech, and stepped a few paces back
from the horse.

It was then that I noticed a small white spot on the horse.
The spot was just above his big troubled eyes. It seemed to
me that there, in the natural parting between the hairs of
his short coat, on the place where the white spot could be
seen, something frightening and terrible was flickering. It
was as though a vulnerable warmth was stirring from those
troubled eyes and vibrating like heat in front of his face. I
saw the gun barrel quite clearly, jutting out of the yellow
stock of the gun which the old man was holding in his trembling
hands. It was aimed straight at this spot. I was terrified.
It was because the big horse was waiting so wonderingly for
what was about to happen.

Then the old man lowered the gun. First he threw a few
stones at the horse, but the animal did not even blink. This
infuriated the old man. He went right up to the horse and

began to pummel his powerful neck. The horse simply shook his head and stood there. Now the old man was really angry. He stamped back to his gun, picked it up, and fired it into the horse's side. Almost immediately one of the forelegs went limp. A sticky red stream coiled down the leg. The horse did not raise his head. He kept it lowered. He stood for a moment and then began to totter. He seemed insecure on his legs. He stumbled a few steps and came to a standstill again. Once again I felt that vulnerable warmth flickering above those troubled eyes. Then a trembling spread through the horse's whole body. He trembled . . . trembled . . . as after an attack of giddiness. The trembling spread, first to the one uninjured foreleg and then to the two hindlegs. Then the trembling began to abate, to sink deep into the body. A second shot rang out over the hills and copses. The white spot on his forehead was now a fount of sticky, somewhat ugly red liquid. The one eye we were able to see slowly lost its grayness. Now its upturned white was washed clean and cold. The old man was still swearing.

"Sonofabitch! sonofabitch!"

We stayed there a long time. The old man sat down. He seemed to be thinking something over, and he was smoking. But when he drew out the blackened knife we knew so well, we left him to do the flaying alone. We walked down the hill and up the next, towards the village. We considered how many pairs of leather slippers old Dojčin would get out of the big horse.

Groups of tired soldiers were passing over the hill. Who knows, perhaps my father was coming with one of them. I ran down the last hill toward home.

META JOVANOVSKI

The Man in the Blue Suit

Nobody could have helped noticing his bright blue suit. He walked upright with steady steps and looked straight ahead and far in front of himself. The rhythms of the lines in the pavement passed beneath his feet, unrecorded.

When he came to the newspaper kiosk, he stopped, but he did not turn. Rigid as a mannequin, he put a hand into a pocket, withdrew a coin, and, after placing it on the counter, turned his head just a bit, only to see which paper he would take. Then he stretched out his hand, folded the newspaper which was given him, and with one motion placed it under his arm and began walking as before, coldly upright, looking far ahead of his steps.

There was a bus stop on the corner, and when he approached it, he raised his eyes in the direction of the board on the post beside it. It was the action of a sensible man.

At the top of the board, above the smaller print, the number 14 was written. The man in the blue suit stopped beneath

---

Meto Jovanovski was born in 1928, in the Macedonian village of Brajčino in the Lake Prespa district, near the Greek border. He was educated at the Teachers' College in Skopje, Macedonia's capital, and taught in a town school near his village and in other parts of Macedonia in the years that followed. Then he took a position in Skopje in a publishing house. During this period he served as editor of *Horizon*, a literary journal. He has also edited *Young Literature* and *The Contemporary*. Today he lives on the side of Mount Nerezi near Skopje with his Serbian wife and their children and is employed as foreign programming director for Skopje Radio–TV. In his back yard is a stone table made from a millstone from his village.

Jovanovski began to publish short stories in 1951, but it was not until 1956 that his first collection, *Jadreš*, appeared. A second collection appeared in 1959, a third in 1971. His fourth and most recent work, a novel, *Frost on the Almond Blossoms*, is

18

it. He moved one leg slightly outward, took his newspaper in his hand, opened it, and began reading.

Meanwhile, the people passing up and down along the street were engaged in the living of their own lives. Some of them glanced at the man in the blue suit, who continued standing just beneath the board which marked the bus stop.

Past the dark entrance of the hospital down the street came two peasants, their bags slung over their shoulders. They walked, silent and bent, looking at the pavement, to the bus stop, where they halted, at the edge of the pavement and a little beyond the man in the blue suit. There they stood, but there was wonder in their eyes, for they were unsure whether it was all right to wait or not.

The man in the blue suit glanced at them, discreetly but questioningly. Then, without hiding his intolerance, he continued his reading. The peasants continued to stand in their places, now almost dozing in the sun, their heads drooping from their thin, hairy necks. But they stood together, at a little distance from the man in the blue suit.

Then the man in the blue suit cast another glance in the direction of the peasants, and this one was less discreet and more disapproving. Now even anger could be seen in his eyes. Holding his newspaper in his right hand, he stretched out his left toward the peasant nearer him. Rather squeamishly he touched the fellow on the shoulder. When

---

now being translated for publication in English. He has also written an historical novella for children.

Skopje, especially since the earthquake of 1963, is a modern Yugoslav city of half a million people, almost a permanent construction site. Yet at the same time it is still very much a Turkish provincial capital, for everywhere, even on the sidewalks of the patterned streets of the new city and beneath the tall new buildings, can be seen the villagers in native costumes, the Albanians in their dirty white skullcaps, the barefoot Gypsies, the trousered Turkish women—all looking a little bewildered and disoriented and unsure. And there are also, of course, the men in business suits. But even many of them are villagers, come only a bit earlier to the city and its brave new world.

the peasant, aroused and confused, turned questioningly toward him, the man in the blue suit said, "Are you waiting for a bus?"

"Yes," said the peasant. Now the other peasant began to be aware that something was taking place.

"Then," said the man in the blue suit, "you must take your place in the queue."

They looked at him in wonder and then lowered their eyes. They did not want to accept what he had said. But they yielded. They moved slightly to stand beside one another.

"When people are waiting for a bus they stand one behind the other and not beside one another," said the man in the blue suit. The two peasants looked at one another and moved to form a proper queue, one behind the other behind the man in the blue suit. Then the man in the blue suit opened his newspaper again and went on with his reading.

The two men behind him stood unmoving but anxious and insecure. It seemed that they would give anything only to be able to turn to one another, to look trustingly at one another; that would explain everything. But they did not dare. They must be content merely to stare at the back of the man in the blue suit.

That man looked at his watch for a moment and then returned to his reading. But when a middle-aged man came to the bus stop, the man in the blue suit took notice of him.

He noticed how impatiently the newcomer walked up and down behind the three in the queue, how he glanced up the street, then straight across it, then thrust his hands in this pockets, and how confused he seemed in his impatience and boredom. Finally, the newcomer turned toward the three in the queue and began to look them over. He moved his eyes from one to the other as if they were notes on a musical scale, until he met the eyes of the man in the blue suit. Then he turned again toward the street and, bending a little, thrust his hands again into his pockets and, bringing his feet exactly together, began to observe the toes of his shoes. The two peasants, expectantly and protesting-ly, looked at the man and then at the man in the blue suit.

"Comrade!" They heard the voice of the man in the blue suit, and felt relieved and lively. The newcomer turned curiously around, not sure to whom the word was addressed. "I think," said the man in the blue suit, looking at him, "that you should join the queue."

The newcomer opened his mouth and gazed at a point in space in front of the speaker. He was preparing his resistance. But when he met the eyes of the man in the blue suit, he said nothing. He only swallowed imperceptibly and moved unwillingly to take his place in the line. The man in the blue suit resumed reading; he did not seem to be at all impatient.

Soon a young man and a girl came. They were very interested in one another—so much so that they did not even notice the queue. They stopped somewhere near the two peasants, the young man listening with attention to the young girl's chatter. The man in the blue suit paid them no attention. The man who now stood last in the queue peered around the peasants toward the man in the blue suit, expecting to see him turn. The man in the blue suit had noticed the couple; he looked at the man at the end as if to tell him that he should take the matter in his own hands. But the man at the end seemed nervous, so the man in the blue suit turned his eyes to the couple and said, "We hope you will observe the queue."

The young man and the girl glanced at the queue and confronted four pairs of eyes and four silent rebukes. They were a bit disturbed, for they wished to be liked. Urged by this wish, they moved to the end of the line, but there they stood beside one another. They would have remained thus, had the man in front of them not continued to eye them. The man in the blue suit turned another page of his newspaper and moved his eyes up and down its columns.

After that, others who came to the bus stop and, out of habit, took random places along side of the others, met the eyes of the men in the front of the line and, finding the imperative of those eyes irresistible, finally took their places in line. Thus, a long queue was formed.

But the bus did not come. The man in the blue suit again looked at his watch and refolded his newspaper. Then he folded the paper again and put it in his pocket. Now he stood still, facing the street, and waited for the bus.

According to the watch of the man in the blue suit the bus should have arrived, but it did not appear. He turned toward the queue. The two peasants were beside him. He said, in a low voice, distinctly, but to no one in particular, "In a civilized town this would never happen."

Only the nearer peasant heard the words, but he turned to his companion and gave him a questioning look. The companion did not even understand that there was something which needed to be understood. He was ready to spit, yet somehow the clean blue sky at which he was staring prevented him from doing so.

Across the street from the bus stop a young man with a large black mustache and a necktie upon which was painted a palm tree and a naked woman stopped and noticed the line of people, so neatly queued up to offer themselves as customers for the city's public transit system. The man in the blue suit noticed his mocking look. Finally, bus Number 14 could be seen approaching.

The people in the line turned to watch it and seemed to be on the verge of moving from their places. The man in the blue suit sensed that the line might shorten or even break now, so he cast his eyes along its length. He tried to meet each pair of eyes along the row, and the people in the queue became quiet.

The bus made its stop so that its entrance door opened exactly in front of the man in the blue suit. He was just about to step up into it when the young man from across the street appeared from around the rear of the bus, his mouth pursed, whistling. With eyes full of irony he stepped ahead of the man in the blue suit. For a moment it seemed that the young man would enter the bus first, but the man in the blue suit put his right arm up and his hand on the side of the rear door and thus blocked his way.

Then the man in the blue suit turned his head toward the peasant beside him and said, "You, please step up." The peasant, amazed, hesitated, not knowing whether it was right to enter the bus or not. "Please, please," the man in the blue suit said to him.

So the peasant stepped up. Immediately, the other peasant followed. The young man from the other side of the street stopped whistling and stared at this keeper of public order. He wanted to push his shoulder against the chest of the man in the blue suit, to force him backwards into the line of entering passengers. But he could not. There was a terrible warning in the man's eyes.

So the young man had to wait. It was very difficult for him to meet the eyes of those in the line, each of whom stared at him with undisguised contempt. So he looked away, toward the entrance of the hospital. He noticed two attendants coming toward him from its back door.

The people in the line slowly entered the bus. The last was a bent old man, whom the man in the blue suit assisted in his long step up. Then the man in the blue suit directed a final glance, full of rebuke, at the young man, turned, and waited to step up into the bus behind the bent old man.

The young man noticed that the attendants were running and were much closer than he expected. In fact, now they were just behind the man in the blue suit. One of his feet was already on the step when he noticed them also. "Do you need me?" asked the man in the blue suit.

Reaching for his arm, which was already grasping the vertical bar at the entrance to the bus, one attendant nodded his head.

"Yes."

"It was good of you to be on time," said the man in the

blue suit. He removed his foot from the step. The young man looked mockingly at him as they turned him away, then he stepped up and into the bus.

"What a strange thing," said one of the passengers who had stood in the queue.

"He seemed so wise," said another.

Several of those who had been waiting in the line turned to stare out the window toward the hospital. There, entering at the dark door, were the two attendants, on either side of the man in the blue suit.

There was a silence among many on the bus. The conductor had not noticed anything unusual, and when the last passenger had entered, he gave the signal for the driver to start.

Dipithon

I. *The First Night*

Well, it was a pretty quiet wedding—no singing and dancing, as they say. Sandrei was married today, without the drummers from Belčište. Just a few people came, for appearance's sake.

The two lovers had been seeing a good deal of each other for the past three months. Those three months had passed quickly, like three winter days. It was a time full of gaiety; songs were sung, music was played—not like these hard times. Those three months had passed like a dream.

The girls from Vrbjane used to sit in the barn at Krume's place, knitting socks; among them was the young Stojna Klimeva, a beautiful girl, pretty as a picture, fresh as a mountain flower on the slopes of Karaorman, slim as a young tree on Slavej. Her eyes were gentle, like rays of spring sunlight caressing the quiet lake; her face was smil-

---

Vlado Maleski was born in 1919 in Struga. He attended primary school in Albania, then went to secondary school in Bitola, the most important town in the region. In 1939 he enrolled as a student at the Faculty of Law in Belgrade (the university for many Macedonians in the period between the wars), but his studies were interrupted by the war. During the occupation he was active in the Macedonian resistance movement and is now serving in the diplomatic corps.

Since the Liberation, Maleski has combined a literary career with a diplomatic one. He has served as editor of *New Day* and of *Vistas*, both important literary magazines, has written two novels—*That Was Heaven* (1958) and *Loom* (1969)—and several volumes of short stories—*George's Crimson* (1950), *Groundswells* (1953), *The War, People, the War* (1967), and *Sons* (1969). His more recent novel, *Loom*, has been acclaimed as a classic of the emergent Macedonian fiction.

ing, her cheeks red and white. And all the girls were smiling. A song would ring out from their laughter:

Hey there, Macedonian, where d'you think you're going? You should be out there fighting, fighting for our freedom.

From time to time Sandrei would come down to the barn. "Come on, girls, faster!" he would say. "Our comrades are barefoot. The girls from Crvenovoda have knitted more than you. We mustn't disgrace ourselves. What d'you think, eh, Stojanka?"

The blood would rush to Stojanka's cheeks and she would answer him with downcast eyes, "We shan't disgrace ourselves."

Sandrei had worked tirelessly all day and every day. Yet he still found time to come and see Stojanka in Krume's barn, where she sat knitting with the other girls.

Everyone who could stand on two feet had been hard at work: the old veterans from the uprising of Ilinden, the youngsters from Debar, women and girls, and children with the five-pointed star on their caps. "Miraculous! miraculous!" the people had said. "May the hand which holds the gun be turned to gold."

But then a terrible disaster struck. Blood was shed in Kičevo, in Preseca, Karaorman, Botun, Turje, Mramorac. Debarca blazed at night, so bright it might have been day. And in this fatal flare, in the reflection of these flames, faces could be seen fiery with unclean blood. Our partisans retreated toward Greece.

Sandrei stayed in Vrbjane. He was to be contact man.

Fog hid the white peaks of Karaorman and Slavej. The people of Vrbjane were heavy-eyed. Smoke rose unwillingly from their ice-fringed houses. The sky was cold and lowering, as were the hearts of Sandrei and Stojanka.

And now tonight—the first night. Both were sitting in the upper room, facing each other, across the loom. Sandrei leaned against the loom and looked around the little room. Stojanka was subdued. Her fingers were passing through the frame among the threads. Rush mats were spread out on the floor. On the rush mats were straw mattresses covered with blankets, white as the mountain snow, and for a headrest there was a brightly colored pillow Stojanka had woven. They did not say a word. The first night. Without singing or dancing.

In the little downstairs room, noise: peasants. Relatives had come to dinner bringing loaves of bread and food with them.

"Well, sister, you lived to see it after all, the marriage of your daughter!"

"God bless the newlyweds, Aunt Andionica!"

"Amen, my child. May God preserve you. I pray He will, with all my heart!"

Upstairs Sandrei stood up, took Stojanka by the hand and bowed low over the tiny silver coins that hung from the wedding ring and, as though to apologize for the starkness of the celebrations, murmured, "It's nothing, Stojanka. Don't be sad. A better time will come some day."

"I'm not sad, Sandrei," Stojanka whispered almost inaudibly.

"It'll be just as it was before. D'you remember, Stojanka? When you used to knit with the other girls in Krume's barn, and when the drummers from Belčiśte used to play for all they were worth, when there were dances in the village? It'll be like that again. And then . . . God will bless us with a tiny child," he added, trembling.

"That's in His hands, Sandrei," answered Stojanka, pressing close against his finely decorated holster. Then she suddenly threw back her head and looked him straight in the eyes.

The little room became filled with a secretive silence. There was a strong, pleasant smell coming from the quince-apples above them in the attic. Sandrei's lungs filled deeply with this smell, which he knew so well from his early childhood. Stojanka smiled at him, as one smiles at a child in the cradle.

Then, suddenly, steps were heard coming up the stairs. The door burst open. When Stojanka saw Krume, pale as wax, the smile died on her lips.

"The Germans are coming, Sandrei. Hide!" Beads of sweat suddenly broke out on Sandrei's forehead. He looked at Stojanka. She was desperate.

"Are you sure, Krume?" he asked imploringly.

"There's no time for talking, Sandrei. . . . I've seen them. Their black guns can be seen in the snow. They must've crossed the little bridge by now. They're either Germans or Albanian turncoats."

Sandrei looked again at Stojanka, and again he asked, "Are you sure you weren't imagining things, Krume?"

"Sandrei, this is no time for fooling around. Hurry! I'm going to warn the others, and you head straight for Mitar's house in Laktinje. We'll meet there." And he disappeared down the stairs.

Stojanka clung round his neck. For the first time he felt the sweet tremor of a girl's face against his own. "Don't be afraid, Stojanka," said Sandrei, plucking up his courage. "They'll just pass through the village, and I'll be back. I'll be back tonight."

He took his revolver from the holster. A blast of wind caught him as he stepped outside. The soldiers appeared before he had even reached Father Siljan's house. He just had time enough to duck behind the apple trees beside the road. He cocked his revolver. . . . Suddenly one of the group lit a flashlight and a pale, haggard face jutted out of the darkness. . . . Dream or reality? Sandrei could recognize the face, it was so close to him. The man was now pointing along the road toward Sandrei's house. "They're our men," he realized with a shock. "They're partisans—that's Pavle!"

"Pavle!" he called in a whisper and stepped out onto the road in front of them.

They looked at each other, long and hard. "You're Sandrei? We were just on our way to your place," the man told him in a low voice.

Sandrei took them up to the empty hayloft by his house. His heart was overflowing with happiness. He could hardly tear his eyes away from them. One moment he would be walking in front of them and the next he would drop back and question them about what had happened to the other comrades, about how they had come from Debarca, and what route they had taken.

Pavle answered him clearly, "Bring us something to eat —anything at all—and then we'll tell you how it all happened. It's four days now since our last meal."

Sandrei dashed back into the house. Some of the wedding guests were still celebrating in the little downstairs room. He entered by the small back door and without making a sound hurried up the stairs to Stojanka. He found her bent over the loom, sobbing silently to herself. When the door opened she gave a start, as if she had been scalded.

"Stojanka!"

"Sandrei. . . . How did you . . .? Run! Hide yourself! They'll catch you!"

"It's our men who have arrived—they're partisans! And I came . . ."

"What about the Germans?"

"No, Stojanka. Krume saw only the guns. It was dark. They are partisans and Pavle is with them."

They sat down again at the loom, in the same position as before. He stretched out his hand and ruffled the bridal veil, which was still on her head. Stojanka's half-opened lips were trembling. Their eyes met. At that moment both of them were thinking the same thought. They were thinking of something dear to them, too dear, something they had once possessed and lost. They had been searching for it for a long time and had lost hope of ever finding it. And now, all of a sudden, they were finding it again.

Sandrei leapt to his feet, and Stojanka rose with him. "We've no time to lose. They're hungry. We must feed them."

"I'll sneak down to the shed and get some bread and

food," said Stojanka. Sandrei took the three bowls and four loaves she gave him to the hayloft.

After the men had recovered their strength a little, they began to talk. Sandrei listened, drinking in every word. He heard all about the life his comrades had been leading in Maglenija, about the great German offensive, about the fourteen days and nights in February without food or sleep, about the fight against the enemy, and about the winter. There had been seventy-five men, altogether. They had been surrounded at Bogomila but managed to fight their way out. Then at night they had been caught in an ambush on the road and cut off from the brigade, which was heading toward Greece. They had held their positions and had managed to draw back across the white mountains to an unfamiliar place. Nineteen of them were frozen to death on the way. Amongst them, clutching his machine gun, was Trpej from Vrbjane, a relative of Stojanka and a great lover of song. It had taken them a whole night to cross the plain of Prilep, and only when they finally reached the hut at Krapej did they rest. Immediately afterwards they had pressed on for the border, making their crossing at Karbunica from where they continued to a hut above Turje and finally ended up in Vrbjane.

Pavle called to Stojanka to come in. A blizzard had begun, and outside, the wind, roaring furiously down from Mount Slavej onto Vrbjane, snatched up the snow from the thatched roof of the hayloft, carried it away high on its shoulders, and then hurled it down again.

"Listen, Sandrei," said Pavle in a hoarse voice, "we're going on again."

"On where?" Sandrei asked anxiously.

"On to Greece. We're setting off in an hour."

"Which route are you taking?"

"None of us knows."

"It's a long journey in snow; you can't do it without a guide," Sandrei mumbled reflectively, almost to himself.

"We know. But you've done the journey often. We thought . . . you might be our guide."

Sandrei stiffened. A raw pain was eating into him, human pain—and the first night? If only he could have one night, just one night on the rush mat, lying on the straw mattress, his head resting on the pillow Stojanka had woven. Three months. . . . Oh, what a time it had been! During that time he had often gone down to Greece as a courier—as far as Saloniki sometimes—a long, hard journey. Whenever he brought the letters, the Montenegrin would greet him with the words, "Bravo, Macedonian!" and he would melt inside with satisfaction. Sometimes Trpej had been in the patrol. It was possible to forget one's difficulties with him. Sometimes they even sang. Ah, Trpej, Trpej. And now? How had Pavle described it? There he was near Bogomila, clutching a machine gun. And he, Sandrei, this evening—the first night—"What is this that flashes through my mind—a sense of guilt?" he thought. "A sense of guilt?" His eyes shone in the dark.

"What do you think?" Pavle broke the silence.

Sandrei took off the bridegroom's scarf that Stojanka had given him in the morning when they came back from church and wiped the beads of sweat from his forehead.

"Yes, of course. Get ready. We're going." And he went off, back to the house, his eyes fixed on the prints he had left a short while ago in the snow.

He stood still for a moment in front of the door to the upstairs room, then he went in. Stojanka was searching for something in a chest, on the lid of which was a crude sketch of a heart surrounding two names, "Sandrei" and "Stojanka." Without turning around she told him: "I'm just taking out a few things for our comrades."

He was silent. He came over to her and stopped still. She straightened up, trimmed the wick on the lamp hanging above the fireplace, and turned around. "What's the matter, Sandrei?" she asked with a smile.

Sandrei looked at her, and she seemed to him even lovelier than when he had met her among the girls knitting at
Krume's barn. And he did not know what to do. He was
overcome by a feeling of gentleness. He would have loved
to embrace her tenderly and tell her everything that had
happened in the hayloft. He longed to talk to her about his
comrades' sufferings, about the snows, about her cousin
who had fallen at Bogomila, but the words stuck in his
throat.

"Sandrei, tell me!" Stojanka begged distractedly.

Then the words were loosened in his throat.

"They ate heartily . . . to the very last crumb. But the
journey. . . . It's a long journey. And barefoot . . . no proper
clothes."

"I've put together a few things from the chest."

Sandrei tried to get a grip upon himself.

"Now they're setting out on their journey for Greece.
And I . . . I must go with them as well." The words seemed
to be torn out from inside him.

Stojanka's expression changed. Tears trickled from her
eyes and ran down her cheeks. She buried her face in her
hands and began to weep silently.

"As their guide, Stojanka. I know the way."

Sandrei's eyes rested for a long time on her black hair.
Then he spoke again. "Stojanka, don't cry. . . . You know
. . . you know . . ."

She uncovered her face and looked at him. "I know, I
know. But . . . it's difficult."

"Difficult," muttered Sandrei. "But I'll come back again.
It isn't my first time. I'll come and . . . I'll bring the spring."

The last guests in the downstairs room were just begin-
ing to leave. Andionica was seeing them off.

"To your health! To your health, my children!"

"Goodbye, Andionica. We'll be coming round tomorrow
for the hot punch!" shouted a raucous voice so that the
couple upstairs should hear. Sandrei and Stojanka looked
toward the window, which seemed in danger of being

carried away any moment by the howling wind.

"You're welcome! you're welcome!" answered Sandrei's mother in a kindly voice, as she leaned against the front door.

Upstairs, after a long silence, Sandrei said, "Take care of Mother till I get back. You'll tell her tomorrow. If anything goes wrong, get hold of Krume."

Stojanka put a loaf into his bag, opened the chest with the heart and two names on the lid, drew out a large bundle, and stood beneath the lamp. With a gleam of sorrow in her eyes she looked down at the rush mat and then put out the light.

Moving silently, so that Andionica should not hear them, they went downstairs and opened the back door. The men were waiting, sheltering themselves against the wall of Krume's house.

"Shall we start?" Pavle asked Sandrei.

"No!" Stojanka's voice broke in on him. "Stop!" There was a catch in her voice. She came over to them, dropped her bundle in the snow, untied it, and took out the wedding gifts she had prepared for Sandrei and the family.

"We had a wedding today. I want to give you presents, comrades. You're going away on a long journey. They're sure to come in handy." They lowered their eyes in silence. Only the blizzard could be heard, howling unceasingly. They were in a row along the wall, so she went up to the first man, a small, stooping fellow, and gave him a pair of socks. Then she passed from one to another, laying the gifts on their shoulders.

They set off. Sandrei lingered for a moment to kiss her on the forehead.

"In a month, Stojanka, we'll all be back. All. We'll stick it out," and he looked across at Krume's barn covered in the deep snow.

"Take care, Sandrei. May God take care of you and watch over you."

Sandrei left her side and hurried off after his comrades.

She watched after them for a while, but the men soon vanished in the snow and darkness. The wind pounced fiercely on Mount Slavej and Karaorman, beating down upon their broad shoulders and tugging relentlessly at Stojanka's wedding veil.

II. *The Day of Smiles*

They were dropped off on the pavement by a car. White. A hand waved through the rear window of the Mercedes— a dark sleeve with three buttons. They entered the house (once the home of an industrialist, the place had long since been taken over by the State). He stamped his boots several times on the Venetian mosaic. With her high heels she did likewise, but less forcefully. As he unlocked a door on the ground floor and let her through first, he caught the whiff of eau-de-cologne—tepid, musty, stale.

"What a day!" Sandrei exclaimed with feeling. "White! And smiling . . . isn't it?"

She was not Stojanka. She was not from Vrbjane and she had never knitted socks for his comrades. And the blood never rushed to her cheeks when she saw him. And her eyes did not wander shyly round the room with the quince-apples, the loom, and the rush mat, because there were no quince-apples, there was no loom and no rush mat. She was an actress. Nada. Sandrei had passed a second first night with her. Moreover, Sandrei was very far away from the dung of the cowsheds in Vrbjane and from Krume's barn. Sandrei was now from Skopje.

Stojanka had remained Stojanka. No longer slim as a young tree on Mount Slavej, but still gentle, with a face that shone like rays of spring sunlight softly caressing the lake.

"Stojanka, I'm in love, Stojanka! At least—I don't really know if I'm in love; in fact I don't even know what it means to say I'm in love. For I did love you, you know. When you used to knit socks in Krume's barn, I did love you. You believe me, don't you? Why should I lie? Why should I spit on the memory of that snowbound barn? But now, you see, something else has turned up! No, no, this one's different, more perfumed, more mischievous. I set off to work, Stojanka, and I know—I'm going to cross over the little wooden bridge, although it takes me out of my way. Then I circle round the building on the left bank of the Vardar, like a horse round a millstone. That's the place where they turn writing into life . . . or . . . yes, the house of tears and songs. Only there, for every song, for every sob, you have to pay."

"I don't understand a word, Sandrei. You frighten me. One can pay for songs, yes, but for tears . . .?"

"I knew you wouldn't understand. Never mind. Ah, yes, once we were together. You said, 'It's like the truth, but it isn't the truth.' Well, that's the building where you said those words, in that building. D'you understand now?"

"When we saw Theodos? The man who fled from the Gypsies and then later became best man to one of them?"

"That's right."

"And the woman who tidied the room on tiptoe so as not to waken him?"

"She too."

"And the man who was in love but was forbidden to love?"

"Enough! Them! In there! Understand?"

Stojanka ran her fingers through the lacy edge of the cloth covering the polished oak table. Her wedding ring with the silver coins clinked dully several times, one after another.

"Stop it!"

Stojanka fell silent. But the ring . . .

"Enough, I'm telling you!" The ring was silenced.

"I'm going to wander round there. And wait. And I know I won't see her. But all the same I'll wait, and then—I'll go away. To work. Like every morning. The Vardar, Stojanka, becomes troubled and muddy before my eyes; it mists over and evaporates, dries up. Only its ribs are left sticking out, like the

ribs of Nasraddin's donkey. Ribs, broken and purulent. The
tall city buildings huddled together, spill over into one another, two into one, three into one, ten into one. They embrace,
kiss, disintegrate, turn into ashes, as it happened long ago
when the fires swept through Debarca. Why? And why do
the people drown with me, with the street, turning gradually,
insensibly, into water and, finally, into vapor?

"Something like what we learned at school, we the half-
educated. But I'm studying, Stojanka. I'm studying now, later
on in life, because I spent my time watching the herds and
then fighting, and nothing came of my early studies. You have
to study; time will crush you, they say, if you don't study.
People were already being crushed, you remember, at that
time. . . . You're crying? Cry. I'll cry too. No, I cannot cry. I
didn't even cry when Pavle told me he had left Trpej in the
snow clutching his machine gun. I didn't even cry when I
wasn't able to lie with you on the rush mat. You cried then
as well."

But it wasn't true. Stojanka had not cried then. She was
not crying now. She was only choking with sobs.

"D'you see now, Stojanka? There is a reason for it all. Despite what has happened. The reason is this: you have stayed
yourself, but I have changed."

"Yes, you are not yourself."

"There! You see what life is like and what it does to people? Am I to blame? Tell me! Speak!"

Maybe he had told all this to Stojanka. Maybe not. More
likely not. He had been going over it all in his head for days
and nights, battling with her in his thoughts. But he had
not told her.

And again he exclaimed, "What a day! White! And
smiling . . . isn't it?"

"Yes," answered Nada as though she had not replied at
all. Now she was standing in her slip (nylon, from abroad)
surrounded by the warmth of the tile stove and her per-
fumes.

He ran his eyes over her. And that flame leapt again inside him, as it had when he first saw her and as it always did whenever she undressed. Even when she did not undress. His feelings hurt him and so too did the wounds of his feelings. His passions burned him and so did the burns on his passions. And the flame constantly flared within him—as it had in the past. Tongues of flame burst out on his skin and in his eyes. And he said, "Like the time when we met, Nada, when the three of us came, with three revolvers . . ."

" '. . . to capture the bandit. My heart was pounding, my blood was boiling. I felt a new joy when I saw you. . . .' And so forth, and so forth! A thousand times! Always the same old song. It's become boring, my dear. Boring."

"Boring? Perhaps it is—always the same old song. But what can I do when I'm madly in love?"

"It's boring, like all repetitions, my dear."

"Repetition. And I so much want to tell you about that day. Today especially. . . . Aha, here's something that hasn't been said. We chased the bandit for five days. For five days and nights we didn't get a wink of sleep or a bite of food. And he—was in town. We picked up his trail. In the building where you lived. On the fourth floor. We came. At the entrance door was a girl with curly, chestnut-colored hair, eyes as dark as Mount Karaorman, in a coat tapered at the waist, thin, transparent stockings and little boots with a fringe of lamb's-wool lining at the top."

"I can recognize myself, my dear."

"I knew you, as though I had always known you. Exactly on this day, at six in the evening. I looked at you and suddenly, a new joy. Well, all right—I don't want to be repetitious. 'Would you mind, comrade,' I said, 'going back to your flat. We've got an important job to do.' You flashed me a strangely beautiful smile. That smile seemed to whisper something quite different from the words I heard: 'I've a performance at seven.' 'You're an actress?' I asked. 'An actress,' you answered. 'If you wouldn't mind waiting all

the same—we'll soon be finished. . . .' You went back to
your flat, and I said to myself as I climbed on up the stairs:
if that man up there on the fourth floor doesn't shoot at us,
I'm going to the theatre tonight. He didn't shoot and I ran
home before seven.''

"I've heard that countless times as well."

" 'Stojanka,' I said, 'get ready. We're going somewhere.'
'What about the child?' she asked. 'Leave him with the
neighbor.' 'You haven't slept properly for ages, Sandrei.'
'I slept at the office,' I lied. . . . We arrived just as the cur-
tain was rising. I didn't watch. I was waiting to see you.
And when you appeared I was blinded. Then Stojanka said,
'It's like the truth, but it isn't the truth.' "

"I've heard that countless times as well."

"I lived in the village, on the fields, in the stables, I
worked as a woodcutter, I cleaned the cowsheds in Vrbjane.
I knew of no other life. If the war hadn't come, I'd never
have known a different life. But it did come. And this is
where it brought me! It brought me here, along with the
fields, the stables, the wood, the cowsheds. . . .''

"And with Stojanka."

"Stojanka. Why should she be to blame because the love
we felt in Vrbjane still burns in her? And why should I be
to blame because I let myself become jealous of modern
youth, unscarred by war, with a carefree, untroubled life
ahead of them? 'Let me live!' I said to myself when I first
saw you. 'I'll lie to my comrades, my friends, my relations.
I'll tell them she makes my life unbearable. Or else that
when I come home tired from work, longing for sleep, for
rest, she talks in her sleep the whole night, gets out of bed,
shrieks, cries bloody murder, hunts for the revolver.' But
I never resorted to this. How could I bring shame to Stojanka, my Stojanka from Vrbjane, because of my troubles?
How could I sully the name of my child's mother? So, all
I said was, 'Let me live!' "

"I've heard that before as well."

"Then once you phoned me, unexpectedly. 'Comrade

Sandrei,' you said, 'I've something confidential to tell you. Will you meet me this evening after the performance?' I waited with the Vardar (but the river didn't wait). I was waiting even before the performance began. You came out after the show, smiling, like an old acquaintance. 'Let's take a walk,' you said. 'Let's do,' I answered, eagerly. 'The whole town's talking about you. The hero of the day!' 'It was my duty,' I told you. 'Modesty?' you asked. 'Duty!' I repeated. 'You've become famous,' you told me admiringly, 'ever since you caught that man on the fourth floor!' "

" 'I saw you at the entrance'—that's what you told me, isn't it? I've heard that as well."

" 'I saw you at the entrance,' I said." He had already told her this. He had gone over it all at least a thousand times, and so he now fell silent. Only his thoughts spoke.

His thoughts. And he? Once again he repeated with feeling, "What a day! White! And smiling . . . isn't it?" By now Nada was lying on the couch, her face covered with a copy of *Politika* opened at the novel page (*A Chess Game* was the title).

"She tells me she was sleeping," he thought. "But I still haven't told her all that has to be said."

"And I have to tell everything. I have to. . . . I'll tell you, Talej, you I know from Vrbjane—a great, song-loving clown who chases away fear with your jokes. I'll tell it to Talej and not to Vlado Maleski who's written nine pages full of lies about me. . . ."

"Truthful lies."

"Lies are lies! Well, I don't know: a wedding without any dance music (there was music, in fact, but not the drummers from Belčište, just our own musicians from Vrbjane), and then the barns, the knitting girls (they were there once, but not then; you lie!). 'And we musn't disgrace ourselves' (I've never made such an inane remark in my life!), and the heavy-eyed people of Vrbjane (all they were interested in was saving their own scalps in those rough times)! And then the loom, the rush mat (the loom, no, the rush mat, yes), and 'It's nothing, Stojanka, don't be sorry. . . . Our time will also come' (how do you know what I said to her in private? Perhaps I only said, 'Lie down,' and perhaps I said nothing at all). 'The Germans are coming!' Krume was supposed to say (they weren't Germans at all. It was just a partisan who came because I was their contact man. He took me to Pavle, the commander. But you write it all up so cleverly, as if it might be a script for a cowboy film!)"

"Shut up, just for once."

"I won't shut up! You lie! Don't you? Ha, ha, ha!"

"That's not true! You want to forget. That's all. You want to crush out the old Sandrei inside you, but Sandrei doesn't give in so easily. Sandrei will always be dragging along with him Stojanka and the child that was not conceived on the rush mat, dragging them and thrusting them in front of the eyes of his conscience, here, surrounded by the smell of eau-de-cologne! Isn't that true?"

"Vlado Maleski's starting to philosophize, isn't he?"

"No. Talej has returned, and Talej is talking to you. But you must understand. Vlado Maleski never renounced Talej. But you want to crush out Sandrei. You want to, but you can't and you never will succeed. And in the end, when all this nonsense has blown over, you'll open your arms to the Sandrei of the first night. It cannot be otherwise."

"Ha, ha, ha! Vlado Maleski acting the wise man again, just as he did when writing about me. But he could also have written about me like this: 'There was a certain Sandrei from Vrbjane. There was a war. Not like other wars. He fought, messed about, did his bit as best he could. He got married, but he didn't sleep with his wife because they would not let him. He had to lead the partisans who had been cut off back to Greece. He felt raw about it, but orders were orders. And the others? They were all the same. There were troubles galore. They had to be borne.' Full stop. Clear and unembellished."

"But the art. . . ."

"Yes, the art. As Stanislavski said, the life. And I wanted to talk about Stanislavski to you. To talk to Talej. Actually, I didn't want to talk about Stanislavski but about the woman lying over there on the couch. She once mentioned Stanislavski. Just like that. Dropped his name in a conversation. I went and read him. The next time it was Shakespeare. I read everything that had been translated—Ostrovski, Molière, Chekhov, Gorki, Priestley, Shaw. I read them to find out something about the theatre. And her—I watch her on the stage. Every day she grows. And I'm happy! I live with her. At last I've found my rest—a true, inner, spiritual peace. . . ."

"True?"

"Yes, and yes again! True peace! Who can contest my happiness? Who? Tell me! Who? Tell me! Come on! Nobody! I'm happy! She loves me. She loves me. Doesn't she? Tell me—speak! She does, doesn't she?"

"She loves you," I said compassionately.

"You see? And I love her. Only now am I beginning to love. When she gets up in the morning—then I can see she loves me. She dresses, looks at me—she loves me. She acts on the stage, she doesn't look at me—yet she loves me. And she calls me 'my dear.' Your lip is trembling in a sneer. If I knew, if I only knew, who said, or even thought, that I'm not happy! I am happy!"

"Why do you keep repeating it?"

"Because there is no happiness without repetition. She doesn't like repetition. And yet she does. She lies. Only it isn't the repetition of words she likes. It's driving."

"Driving?"

"By car. I don't have a state-owned car. I'm too far down the ladder. But my manager's a good fellow. He likes us. Nada need only drop the hint and my good comrade takes us out in his car. Off we go, roaming and roving. Up hill and down dale. Nada likes people to know down there by the Vardar that she . . . goes driving. Women! Today we were in Ohrid. There was snow on Babuna as there always is at this time. Thick snow. Blizzards. We went up to the mountain pass. A blizzard. And I could hear something crying in the swirling snow, in the midst of the grayness above us. You couldn't even see a step in front of your eyes. Like the time when the wind was blowing like a demon from Slavej and Karaorman. Maglensko was far away. The land was far away. Nothing but snow all round. We staggered along, frozen to the teeth. 'How much more?' they asked me. 'Just a little farther,' I lied. And the land was far away, so too was the brigade, so were the comrades. And farther still was the rush mat on the floor. . . . Nada whispered into my ear, 'My dear!' If only I knew who said, or even thought, that I am not happy!"

No, he did not tell me any of this. He only went on repeating, wearily, thoughtfully, almost inaudibly, without any conviction: "What a day! White! And smiling . . . isn't it!"

"Yes," I said, as though I had not said anything at all.

KOLE ČAŠULE

A Macedonian Girl

Original title, *Compatriots**

"Evening, brother," said the girl—in the old language. She was sitting down beside me in the Canadian bar.

"I've got no money," I told her, stiffly.

"So what," she said. Just like that. And she was from my own country across the sea. "I know what love is," she said.

I know your kind of love, I thought. But I wasn't going to get into that. She'd only get angry.

"You're a knockout," she said. "A real knockout."

I grinned. What else could I do?

She won't hang around long, I thought. She'll see I'm not standing her any drinks, so she'll sit around for a while

---

* *Editor's Note:* The new title of this story is also the title of a well-known and highly sentimental Macedonian folk song.

Kole Čašule was born in Prilep in 1921, and, until interrupted by the war, he studied medicine at the University of Belgrade. Since the war (in which he took an active part) he has occupied various cultural and diplomatic positions, including an assignment to Ottawa, and he has established himself a writer of short stories and plays. He has also been employed as an editor, as a director of Skopje Radio, and as Director of the Macedonian National Theatre. *Share in the Wind* (1956) and *Crnila* (1962) are among his most celebrated plays.

The immigrant worker from Yugoslavia is familiar throughout the world today, and perhaps an unusual number of these workers are Macedonian in origin. For several hundred years now it has been a part of the life of the Macedonian villages and towns to see the able-bodied men depart—for a season, a number of years, or a lifetime—to seek work in foreign lands. Their experience—the longing of the emigré for his homeland, his sense of loss, or the anticipation of his return at home—has

and then push off. I really didn't have any money left. I
was down to the last ten dollars of my pay, and I was
damned if I was going to blow it on her.

"Well, how about it, huh? Aren't you going to stand me
a drink? You're as tight as a . . ., oh, never mind."

She's angry, I thought. I'll have to stand her a drink.

"I've got no money," I told her.

"Who's asking you for money?" she demanded, raising
her voice. "I don't give a damn about your money. Besides,
if I was after money, I wouldn't come to you."

"You need money to buy drinks," I said. This, I knew,
was my last card.

"And you need a little class," she replied. Then she
lifted a leg, pulled up her skirt just like they do in the
movies, pulled out a ten-dollar bill from the top of her
stocking, and threw it down in front of me. "There's your
money! Now stand me a drink." The barman smiled know-
ingly.

I felt uneasy. They've been cooking up something between them again, I thought.

"Come on, stand me a drink!" she said.

"There's no point." I pushed the ten dollars back to her.

"Why not?" And without bothering to wait for my
answer she continued, "Because it's me who's paying?"

I nodded. What the hell did I want to come in here for,
I thought, cursing my luck. Why did I have to pick on this
place?

"Forget it," she said, and she put away the bill. "What'll
you have? I'll have a double scotch on the rocks."

So—she was still trying. And now with my money,
what's more.

As if I didn't know what a double scotch on the rocks
was. She was up to something, I was sure of that. But what

---

been dramatized in countless Macedonian folk songs and has
been a recurring theme in more formal literature. So Čašule's
story treats of a subject very familiar to the Macedonian reader.

was she after? "I'm doing fine." I said. I pointed to the unfinished bottle of beer in front of me.

"Beer? How the hell can you drink that stuff?"

"It's cheaper." I shouldn't have said that. It probably
would rile her.

She gave me a low look. "You're a knockout, I'm telling
you. A real knockout."

I kept quiet and tried to smile. She isn't cross, I thought.
Seems like she's not done too bad today. She isn't cross.

"All right," she said, "I won't have a double scotch on
the rocks. Get me a Canadian Club. Have one yourself. It's
great with beer. Which beer are you drinking?" She turned
the bottle round and looked at the label. "You must be . . .
never mind what. How can you drink this horse piss? Don't
let me ever catch you drinking it again."

I ordered two Canadian Clubs. "Take your money," I
told her. "I've got enough for two Clubs."

"So, you want to get rid of me, eh?"

"No," I said. "No, I don't."

"You're lying."

I was silent. The waiter brought the two Clubs. I took
out my last ten and paid. Once the bartender had gone,
I whispered to her softly, "That's the end of my pay."

"Come on!" she said. I could see she simply wasn't paying attention to what she was saying. She had fixed her
eyes on a tall, red-haired man who was coming into the bar.
I took a drink. "D'you see him?" she asked. "That red-
haired guy? He's rolling in money."

Then suddenly, out of the blue, she asked, "Does your
wife write to you?"

What the hell's she getting at now? I wondered. "Now
and then," I answered.

"Fool."

I had no idea which of us she meant.

"Order another two."

I ordered the drinks and made a swift calculation. Only
six dollars and eighty cents left.

"He won't give me the slip," she said. "Not on your life he won't. He owns three buildings, old lobster there does. And seven hundred a month in salary. You can't even begin to imagine what that's like," she said.

"No, I can't," I said, to make her happy.

"Of course you can't. You'd go out of your head if someone gave you seven hundred dollars a month. That's for sure."

Just give me seven hundred dollars a month, I thought, and we'll see if I go out of my head or not.

"Really," she said, downing her second whiskey. "What would you do if you suddenly started earning seven hundred dollars a month?"

"I'd know what to do, if I could just get my hands on it."

"No you wouldn't," she said. "You aren't the money-making kind, believe me you aren't."

That's only because I don't have any, I thought.

"You know, friend," she went on, staring more and more aggressively at the red-haired man, "you could. . . . Take my hand!" she said. "Take my hand when I tell you! Go on! More gently, you fool! more gently! Take my hand as if you were trying to talk me into something, Numbskull!"

"I don't get you," I said. I really didn't understand what she was after.

"It doesn't matter," she said. "You're a . . . oh, the hell with it! I picked you up. Listen, now. Listen carefully." She leaned over and began whispering in my ear. "Look into my eyes as if you were in love with me. Smile. Smile a little, dammit! Ooooh!"

She's gone crazy, I thought. But, of course, I did as she told me. Why make her angry?

"Pretend you're trying to talk me into something. Understand?"

"I don't understand a thing," I told her. "But don't worry, I'll do as you say."

"You've always been stupid, believe me."

All right, so I'm stupid. You should have thought of

that earlier. I looked at her, smiled, and stretched out my
hand as if I wanted to grab her around the waist.

"Don't start getting ideas," she said.

"I'm not getting any ideas," I answered. Not bloody
likely, I thought, coming to myself.

"Order another two Clubs," she told me.

"Maybe you'd better slow down," I said.

"Come on! Order the drinks!"

She was going to get drunk, I knew. But what could I
do? I ordered the drinks.

Five dollars and twenty cents. Twenty cents less for the
tip. That leaves an even five. Just great.

"You'll get drunk," I told her.

"No I won't!"

You'll get drunk, I thought. I know you. You'll get drunk
on my last ten dollars, and what'll it all come to in the end?
Nothing.

I cast a glance at the red-haired man. My God, I thought,
he's fallen for it. How about that! "I'll get my cut?" I whispered to her.

"It depends," she said. "Squeeze me a little. A little
more. Lift that great paw of yours higher, for God's sake!
That's right."

"What does it depend on?" I asked.

"On you," she answered.

I really didn't know what she meant. On me? How?

"On you," she repeated, without offering any explanation. What business was it of mine? "Now try to give me
a kiss," she told me. "When I slap you across the face, you
jump back."

"What's this about slapping?" I asked, trying to shake
her off.

"Don't try to back out of it now," she muttered through
her clenched teeth. "You're not going to budge from here,
get it?"

No, I thought. No, I won't. I'm getting out of this. I don't
like it. The cops here are on to you before you can turn

your head. For the first time I spoke my thoughts aloud:
"I won't."

"Why not, meat-head?"

"I don't want any trouble with the cops." That was the
truth. You could get a pretty stiff sentence for molestation.
Six months at least. No, I wasn't going to get mixed up in it.

"What d'you mean, cops! There's no cops for miles
around, you idiot. Squeeze me round the waist. Hard."

The red-haired man got up and went to the gents. "He
was drinking before he came here," she remarked. She
pushed me away from her. Now she's beginning to get
angry, I thought. Why the hell did I have to come in here?
What shall I do? I looked at her. She was angry.

"You're a fool," she said, "a prize fool."

"I'm afraid," I said. "I've just landed myself a job and
I don't want to lose it." I really was afraid. Why should I
run the risk of losing my forty dollars a week? It was my
best pay since coming to the country, and I certainly wasn't
going to throw it away just like that. No, I thought, I won't.
I looked at her and repeated aloud, "I won't."

"There's nothing to be afraid of," she said. "I know the
cop on the beat round here."

I don't believe it, I thought.

"I know what I'm doing," she said.

"All right, what's the game?"

"I want to make him jealous," she said. "It's the best cure
of all."

"And?"

"And what?" she retorted. She looked at me and began
to laugh. "And then we start feeding him a line."

"I'm just asking," I said.

"And I'm giving you the answer," she replied. "You
know, brother," she added without pausing, "Canada's
really taken the shine off you. Honest to God."

It isn't true, I thought. "I'm not so sure," I said.

"Of what?"

"Of what you were just saying."

"Oh drop it, for God's sake. As if I don't know you. Don't you remember during the war when Captain Gruya cracked you so damn hard across the face in front of the whole platoon? I was really sorry when that happened, believe me. Not for any reason—just because you're so stupid."

Yes, I thought, but now Captain Gruya's pushing up the daisies, and I'm still around. But I didn't say anything to her. I knew her too well. She'd run off and babble to somebody, and then. . . . So I kept quiet. I'm not stupid.

"You know what's wrong with you?" she asked.

"No."

"You want to be honest, that's what's wrong."

I didn't understand her.

"You don't understand, do you?"

"No, I don't."

"There. You see?"

"I don't see," I said.

"It doesn't matter. That's the peasant coming out in you. You peasants are the only people who still believe that something called honesty exists in this world. Isn't that a laugh? You're the only ones who believe in it, and everybody looks on you as being thoroughly dishonest. That's why you always come off second best. That's what's wrong with you."

"I'm not a peasant," I said. And that's the truth. My family moved into the city a good fifty years ago.

"Yes, you still are. In a way."

"Not in any way," I said huffily.

"Yes, you are. Stop thinking about it. You'll tire yourself. Anyway, it's of no importance. Look, there he is—he's coming back. Watch out." The red-haired man walked into the room.

"How are you off for women?" she asked. She smiled.

"So-so." I answered.

"How's that girl of yours—you know, the one that's nine feet tall? What the hell is she anyway, Ukrainian?"

"I'm not living with her any more."

"Kicked you out? So soon?"

I didn't answer. It doesn't matter, I thought; she isn't really listening to me. But she kept on with her questions all the same.

"Where are you living now? I mean where are you staying?"

"All over." I'm not such a fool as to tell you where, I thought. I don't want you coming around to plague me some night, drunker than you are now.

"You're lying," she said. "You're afraid of me coming around and bothering you."

"Honest . . ."

"Come stay at my place," she said, breaking in. "We'll split the rent. Which shift d'you work?"

"Second shift."

"Pity it isn't the third. It'd suit me better."

I've got a good mind to do it, I thought.

"Now give me a hug," she said.

"Just leave out the slapping, if you don't mind." I reached out for her.

"Tell me, how much d'you think he's carrying on him?"

"It depends," I said.

"A lot or a little?" she demanded.

"It depends," I said.

"What's it depend on? To hell with you and your damn depending. Order two more Clubs."

"You've had enough," I said.

"No I haven't."

I ordered. Inside I was mad at myself. I'd end up by wasting all my money on her. It was time to get up and leave. Yes, I thought, I must just get up and leave. What can she do to me? Nothing.

The waiter placed our order on the table.

Three dollars and sixty cents, less thirty-five cents tip, that leaves exactly three dollars and a quarter. If I don't get up now, I thought, I won't have anything to eat tomorrow. And there's still three whole days till my next pay.

The red-haired man seemed to be winking, or was it just

my imagination? I tried to work out how much I had drunk. Three Clubs and two beers. It was beginning to go to my head. It was time to stand up and leave.

"He's looking," she said.

"He's looking," I said. And I started thinking. It wouldn't really be fair to leave her just at this moment. Not now that things are beginning to go our way. After all, we both come from the same country. She's got a right, poor thing, to make her buck.

"If it all works out well you'll get ten per cent," she said.

"I'll what?" I swallowed my words and began calculating. Even at fifty dollars I'd still be losing. It'd be a good thing only if he has at least a hundred on him. Or even better, two hundred.

Nonsense, I thought. Nobody even in this damned country strolls around with two hundred dollars in his pocket. Not even on payday. "It's pretty little," I said.

"That's all," she said. "No more."

I felt it was time to order. I called for two more Clubs. "You'll get drunk," she said.

"No I won't."

"Yes you will. I know you. You can't hold your liquor."

"No I won't," I whispered, snuggling up closer to her. Well, I thought, she isn't really so bad to look at. And she used to be . . . Ah, she was really something when we crossed Caravanka. She even got to Vienna. Those breasts! Now they're pretty sloppy. And those legs . . . wow!

"Take it easy," she said. "You're going too fast. He might get disgusted. Slow down."

"It doesn't matter," I said.

"Of course it matters."

It's a shame, I thought. She might have made somebody a good wife. A wife to go out with on Sunday, to go to church with, to walk along the main street with.

"I'm going to pretend to go to the ladies room," she said. She slipped out of my grasp.

Pity, I thought as I watched her walking away. Pity. Pity.

And I started thinking of my own wife. Foolishness. I took
a drink. Then I ordered another one on the spot, for myself.
It doesn't matter, I thought. I'm not going to make any
more calculations. The future can take care of itself.

"Another beer!" I shouted. "Make it a Molson!"

"Coming," called the barman.

I began inspecting the red-haired man. Where the hell did
she get the idea of calling him lobster?

"It's a laugh," I said to myself aloud. I spit on all this.
He must be some fool of a Scotsman. Look at his face. Like
a melon soaked in red wine. What does he do with his seven
hundred dollars? What does he spend it on? I bet it all goes
like this, on whores. Or else he drinks it up. Some life. I
mixed the whiskey into the beer.

What would I do if I made seven hundred dollars a
month? I'd buy a house. What the hell do I need a house
for? I could earn another seven hundred dollars anyway
on houses. What then? I'd divorce my wife. No. Yes, I
would. I'd invite her over here. She wouldn't like it here.
No, no I wouldn't get a divorce. I'd leave her just where she
is. And I'd send her a hundred dollars a month. What'd she
do with a hundred dollars? What'd she spend it on? There's
nothing back home for her to spend it on. I'd send her fifty
a month. Even fifty's a lot. Hold on, let's work this out. I
took a drink and began calculating. "It's a lot," I said aloud.

The waiter came over. "Yes?"

"Nothing, my friend, nothing," I said. You big thug, I
thought. You've been flapping your ears again. I looked up.
She was coming back. "How goes it?" she asked. She sat
down.

"O.K." Her suggestion was still worth giving some
thought to, I decided. It really would work out cheaper for
both of us. And what business was it of mine what she did
or how she lived? It was her life. And I wouldn't even have
to pay for it. Doesn't that take it all?

She interrupted my thoughts. "Now you go to the gents."

"Why?" I asked.

"Never mind why," she said. "Just go."

I walked past the lobster. What a nose! I thought as I went into the lavatory. How much rent does she pay for that room of hers? It can't be more than seven or eight dollars. Strange, who'd have thought I needed a piss so badly. I guess one could live with her after all. Of course she's a bit headstrong, but then what woman isn't. Anyway, it's got nothing to do with me. She's herself and I'm myself.

An old man came into the lavatory. What a terrible thing old age is, I thought. It makes a monster of you the moment your back is turned. Who knows what sort of an Adonis he was as a young man. Now look at him. He can't even hose down the trough properly.

I went back to the bar. The red-haired man was sitting beside her. In the place where I had been sitting. So soon? I wondered. And now? What was going to happen to me? She hadn't told me anything. I'll go over to them, I decided. My money's still on the table.

I started, walked slowly, pretending my legs weren't steady.

"Oh," I said. "A new friend. Glad to meet you. My name's Stanov." I could have kicked myself. Why the hell did I have to let him know my real name? Why? Why? I tried to sit down.

She called the bartender.

"Waiter."

"Three more Canadian Clubs," I said when the bartender came.

"This man's annoying me," she said. "Clear him out of here, will you? You can't even have a quiet drink with a friend because of creeps like him."

"Hey! Wait a minute!" I said.

"Haven't you got an appointment?" asked the lobster.

"*Mulim vas?*" I said.

"I don't understand him," said the lobster to her.

I had forgotten that he didn't understand Serbian, so I repeated the question in English. "Are you asking me if I've got an appointment?"

"Yes, you," he said quite simply and openly.

"Me?" I asked.

"You," he said. Then, without a flicker of hesitation, he added, "don't you get it?"

I winked at her. "So, he's the one, is he?" I asked.

"How d'you like that for nerve," she said. "He even winks at me."

"Mike!" shouted the lobster to the bartender. "If you don't throw this drunk out, we're leaving."

"Steady, steady," I said. "Misunderstanding."

"How long do I have to put up with this?" she asked. The lobster stood up. He reached for my jacket. Oh, no you don't, mister, I thought. Nobody touches me, and you're not going to either. I raised my fist. I was going to let him have it right in the kisser.

What happened?

"What happened?" I asked again, this time aloud. And I looked around me. I was lying in the street. A few people were standing around me. A cop was running up towards me from the other end of the street.

"Why do they drink when they can't take it?" asked one of the bystanders.

Just look at the swell coat he's wearing, I thought. He went on talking about something.

"They shouldn't be allowed to serve drinks until they've seen the money," said another.

"I paid for everything I drank. I even paid for hers as well."

"He's drunk," said the man in the coat.

Then I saw the old man from the gents. What's he going to say, I wondered. I smiled at him.

"We've met before—in the lavatory," I said. He turned around and went away.

"Get up," said the policeman.

"Of course," I said, and I got up.

"Break it up now," he said to the crowd. They slowly began to drift away. "What's all this?" he asked me. "Threw you out, did they?" Then, without even waiting for an answer, he said, "You wait here till I come back," and he walked into the bar.

Not a bad cop, I thought. He wants to get at the whole truth. He ought to. After all, what's the government paying him for? But while I was still thinking about this, I remembered her words: "I know what I'm doing." She really did. Why the hell did she have to go and pick on me with all these Canadian fools around.

The cop came back.

"Beat it," he said. "Get lost. And don't let me find you on my beat again, or I'll run you in."

"Hold on," I said. "Hold on, will you. Let me explain. I didn't do anything wrong."

"I know," he said. "So beat it."

Who knows what kind of a story they fed him in there.

"She and I—we're from the same country," I said, just for the sake of saying something.

"You don't say," he replied.

I better shut up, I thought.

She came out of the bar with the lobster, arm in arm. "Ask her," I said to the cop.

He asked her, half mockingly. "This guy here says you're his friend; he says he's from your country." He's very polite all of a sudden, I thought. They're all in league—the lot of them.

She turned around, looked at me over his shoulder, and shouted, "From my country, huh? Him? That's what they all say." She went off with the lobster.

"Beat it," said the cop.

No choice, I thought. So, of course, I made myself scarce. What's all this mean? I wondered. And I answered the question myself.

To hell with the lot of them. I'm broke. Then I added,

aloud, "Why did they have to pick on me? Goddam 'em."
Everything would be different, I knew, when I sobered up.
I set off for home.

I'll write to my wife. I'll write her a long letter.

To hell with my wife, to hell with them all. I'm going to
the Ukrainian girl. It's always good with her. Then I won't
have to worry about food, at least till next payday. I passed
another cop and greeted him most politely. He wasn't the
same one, but it made no difference, no difference at all.
Absolutely no difference.

Early Evening

She had been prepared to hear almost anything but that. She had, in fact, been expecting quite the opposite, for having observed them for so long—she did not see how anything could have escaped her notice—it did not seem that anything of significance could have passed between them. Or was it simply that she was not capable of seeing anything significant?

She had, of course, never been close to her sister. They were always quarreling over the pettiest trifles and often exchanged sharp words. Now, it would seem foolish for her to pay too much attention to what she had seen.

Yet she was disturbed, although she sensed that he might be mortally offended if she were to make the slightest mention of it. She was certain what his reaction would be, even though he, partly because of his age but even more because of the kind of life he had led, always accepted her jests in the same spirit in which they were given, with a steady smile and a teasing shrug, then a swift turning of conversation to some quite different topic.

For his part, even he was surprised when he heard from

Cvetko Martinovski, a writer and journalist in Skopje, where he was born in 1930, has edited several literary magazines in Skopje and is now an editor in the Nova Makedonija Publishing Company. His own published work includes two collections of short stories, both of which appeared in the late 1950s.

The practice of visiting monasteries on saints' days is a longstanding folk tradition in Macedonia, today honored mainly by the middle-class citizens of the city. Often these saints' days become little country fairs as well, with the visitors sleeping under the stars to prolong their holidays into the next day. But perhaps a better sense of these little festivals can be obtained from reading Martinovski's story.

his own lips the words which marked the end of a period
in his life, a period he had scornfully called his youth. He
had even built up something like an opinion of his own
about this, a kind of personal philosophy he would often
slip into the conversation with a joking smile when chatting
to his friends, or especially to her, the older sister, who had
now, oddly enough, become his companion for the remain-
der of his life. "There is no such thing as old age," he would
often declare (he was never sadder than at moments of
transition). "There is only youth—dewy youth, budding
youth, blossoming youth, youth past its full bloom, fading
youth, the final traces of youth, the beginnings of old age.
Old age does not exist, is it not so, my old maid? Or perhaps, as an aging girl, you do not agree with me?" Still, in
his own words, he was at the age of youth past its full
bloom, and she was the same age.

They had met quite by chance and, without knowing why,
had struck up a friendship—without expectations, without
sentiment, sometimes even without interest. Yet each was
quite satisfied by the other's presence, as though they were
long-time companions and not a couple newly in love.
Sometimes they were quite ready simply to stop seeing each
other (as was often the case in their relationships with
others), without feeling any longing, any anger, or any
reproach. They never discussed their relationship with one
another, and it is not likely that either of them gave any
thought to its eventual outcome. Since he was not adept at
striking up acquaintanceships with women, she became for
him only a means toward the fulfillment of a need, almost a
habit which he found in some ways humiliating and slightly baffling. There were times when he even laughed at himself for having allowed this improbable relationship to go
on for so long; there were times when it struck him that he
ought to break it off. But he constantly postponed this decision in the expectation of meeting some woman who would
attract him more powerfully. Naturally, it never occurred
to him that by staying with her he was losing all his freedom

and thus forfeiting his chance of establishing a new relationship. Because of his indifference and lack of keenness he simply was not aware of opportunities. He was accustomed to her almost as though she were his wife, and she knew instinctively and unresentingly whenever she was unwanted or in the way. He, in turn, never felt any resentment when she was unable to be with him as he would have liked.

She had already had a number of affairs and had given up all thought of marriage. She had perhaps determined to avoid the desperate decision, and perhaps that resignation was basically no more than another facet of the restless, headstrong impulsiveness which drove her from one affair to another. Perhaps it was her rebellion against a premature insistence on the need for marriage.

Moreover, she was reconciled to the fact that after this affair with him (which had now lasted long enough to be no longer noticeable) there would be only two possibilities left to her. She could either withdraw completely into spinsterhood, or she could abandon herself, as several of her friends had done, to an affair with the first man she happened to meet. And this could only satisfy a present need; inevitably it would leave a backwash of disenchantment and a vapid sense of hollowness.

Sometimes her younger sister would go with them to the cinema or to the beach. The younger girl was very friendly toward him, and yet she retained a certain reserve, as though he were a stranger, as though she had just met him on the previous day. But despite this reticence one could feel that she worshipped him, that she was ready to do anything for him. Her elder sister even occasionally suspected that the girl had become enamored of him. This would not have surprised her, because she herself was not "in love." The younger sister had not yet "fallen in love," although she was already grown.

Yet there was always that curious mixture of flippancy and intimacy with which he treated her. Often, when he wanted to needle her, he would call her a child. And this, for the younger girl, was the greatest possible offense. At the very suggestion she would bristle, withdraw into herself, and wait impatiently for the first opportunity to call her sister an old spinster in his presence. And when this happened the elder sister would observe his reaction closely, always conscious that she was losing much in his eyes because of her younger sister's presence. But she always quickly realized that nothing would be achieved by anger, and so she would answer back jokingly, taking care to hide her malice, pouting playfully, and covering up her vexation by calling her sister "babyface," "little brat," "monkey," "tiny-tot," or the like.

He took great delight in these little squabbles of theirs and, by pretending ignorance, would encourage them with seemingly innocent remarks, taking care never to side with either of them. He would laugh roguishly at their barbed words. But then he would disengage abruptly, as if some weighty thought had suddenly occurred to him. His face would darken. Then the older sister would feel that he was distancing himself from her—if, indeed, he had ever felt close to her at all.

She was normally never at a loss for words, and yet, whenever he saw them home, she would always stop by the front door and thank him with the same set phrases (he already knew them all by heart and would occasionally take the words right out of her mouth: "Thank you very much for . . .") before going into the house.

Although these playful tiffs between the two sisters were frequent and spirited, and although they believed that they were not "close," until that evening nothing had ever seriously come between them. But that evening they were both conscious that something had happened to change things irredeemably, something all three of them would prefer to forget.

*   *   *   *

It was very much the custom to visit the monasteries on the eve of a great saint's day. A small group of friends would arrive early in the evening, carrying guitars and accordions, food and drink. All through the night, until the face of darkness began to pale, there would be singing and dancing. The peasants from the nearby villages always came with their shepherd's pipes, their lambs, and the big round loaves which they carried in brightly colored shoulder bags. One could stroll among the stalls with their trinkets and bric-a-brac. Everyone was at his ease, without reserve or defensiveness. Everything one did—lying on the monastery lawn with the stars glittering above one's head (closer, somehow, than one ever saw them elsewhere), joining in the ring of dancers, teasing one another with the trinkets at the stalls, with the cheap brooches and toys, stealing caresses among the trees—everything left one with a memory of freshness, innocence, and joy. This, at least, was how he recalled those evenings.

So it was that as the next saint's day approached, he proposed making an excursion to a nearby monastery. He had never taken her on such an excursion; he had always gone with other friends. He really felt that if it did not live up to his expectations a wound would open in his memory that would be a constant source of regret to him.

It was early autumn, that brief, gentle Indian summer which can be felt more in the changing colors than in the freshness of the air. Burdened with a haversack—as he put it caustically, with enough food to feed an army—he set off with his friend at a merry pace, and he welcomed the younger sister, who had unexpectedly joined them. The excursion was for him the fulfillment of a long-standing wish. Perhaps by chance, perhaps not, they even took the wrong turning and found themselves straying down some curious little paths, which branched off into a network of tracks running through vineyards. It seemed to him almost as if these tracks were laughing with him as he stopped, from time to time, to light a cigarette or take a sip or two from the small brandy flask.

Toward evening, through the poplars, they caught sight of the dark domes of the monastery church. They seemed only then to have noticed the peaceful cries of the crickets. A strange sense of relief followed, as though a gentle hand were caressing them. They felt far removed from the grimy quotidian world of the city. Here, with the last flush of the setting sun streaking through the branches of the trees, under the shadow of the encircling hills, life seemed so simple and sensible. This was not the place for exchanges or memories of small hostilities, even for those secretive murmurings which can so provoke one with the thought that one's life has been vain, useless, empty, and sham.

The monastery courtyard was already teeming with people who had arrived earlier. From under the large trunk of an old tree could be heard the sounds of a guitar playing to a large circle of people; here and there candles could be seen flickering like restless fireflies. The whole scene seemed almost unreal, as though it were part of an old, well-known, but long-forgotten tale.

They made themselves comfortable in the shelter of an old barn with broken floorboards. While the two sisters prepared the salad for dinner by the flickering light of the candles, he thought with satisfaction that everything was perfect, so perfect that he did not want to disrupt this strange, undulating flow of thought which had been set in motion by the sight of their tomato-stained hands and then diverted by the thought of the older sister who, he was sure, would remain unmarried. He began to recall with sorrow all those attentions she had shown him. This led him to the provoking fact that he too was in some way isolated, living from one day to the next without ever feeling that anyone was really close to him. And so his thoughts flowed on through all the experiences of his life as if rolling back through a heavy fog. But one of these recollections caused him to frown.

Who knows why just this one had to leap out of his memory.

It had happened in the city on a filthy night that seemed to him centuries removed from the present. That evening he had bumped into a good friend of his in a café. They had knocked back quite a few drinks. As they were leaving the place he had caught sight of a woman he knew, one of those who aren't particular about the company they keep. Whether it had been out of some youthful urge to prove to his friend that he knew people from all walks of life, or whether it had been out of mere boredom was not clear. At all events, he had called out to her. His friend, who was older and who had already been through a good deal of this sort of thing, had given him a reproachful look when he explained the girl's profession, had caught him by the arm, and had steered him over to the café on the other side of the road. Here they had gone inside. But no sooner had they ordered their drinks than the girl's head had appeared against the misty windowpane. He had felt ashamed of what he had done a few minutes earlier and had been seized with panic at the thought that she might come into the café. He had leapt up, as though struggling for breath, and had rushed outside just as he was, without his coat. She was not alone. There was another woman with her. Furious at himself, and apparently having forgotten that it was he who had called her over, he turned on her roughly as if to ask her what she thought she was doing there.

"What do you want with me? Are you trying to . . .?"

"Nothing! If I'm not mistaken it was you who called to me a short while ago." She looked at him in astonishment before turning away. He had never before behaved like this. Although he had spoken to her quite casually, her rebuff infuriated him. Perhaps this anger was partly due to the brute in him, which stirred up painful thoughts and reminded him that he had never had such a woman and had never even been desired by one. But now—to be given the cold shoulder by a woman like that, a prostitute. . . . He had struck rock bottom. And then there was the sharp pang of his awareness that he had allowed himself to be humiliated in front of her friend. He stared at the other woman. She was young, still a child, "not a day over sixteen," he reckoned at a rapid glance.

Then, unconsciously softening his voice, he spoke to her and asked her simply, "How about it?"

It was not entirely clear at first whether she had been serious when she answered simply, with perhaps a touch of shyness, "Well, . . . O.K."

Now that she had accepted his offer, his self-esteem strangely returned to him. But what was there to do? His friend was waiting for him in the café. What was there to do? He had also left his coat inside the café. After a brief moment of reflection he simply caught her by the hand, and they set off together in search of a place. The other woman, whom he had also known, followed her friend—after them like a shadow. They turned down the first alley. He remembered that there had been an unfinished building not far away. They entered the empty site. He was seized by a wild fever as he felt her firm, young body, her breasts neat and round beneath his fingers. He was almost maddened by desire. It was not so much because he had such a woman as because of something animal hidden within him, an insatiable thirst for something needed on the threshold of maturity. He had not recalled seeing this girl in the company kept by her friend. "A newcomer," he thought, somewhat scornfully, and then, with a certain wild determination, he flung his jacket onto the dirty concrete and stretched himself out hungrily over her. Not even this was enough for him. He wanted to feel her whole body. And so with desperate foolhardiness— he did not wish to think of the diseases she might have—he took her. He did not know if she was aware of the fact that, over by the entrance, like some mocking, contemptuous guard, stood the other girl. Then he returned to the café covered in dirt. His friend smiled, but said nothing. He had felt grateful to him for this.

"You're miles away. What are you thinking about? Look, you haven't even touched your wine. There, how was the salad?" He nodded distractedly, shook his head to clear away the memory and then, with a forced smile, threw an arm over their shoulders and suggested they take a walk.

"What about the things? Somebody might steal them. She'd better stay behind," said the older sister.

The younger girl stiffened a bit, but then stuck out her tongue. He gave a good-natured smile and, although he regretted that the two of them could not go off on their own —he would have liked a few moments of intimacy with her —he made a gesture of comprehensiveness and placed a hand on each one's shoulders. They set off without a word. The younger sister, now smiling, looked at him with a strange intensity that he found rather pleasing and then told them, "I'll soon leave you alone." There was something in her voice which assured them that she would indeed soon go back; with almost a laugh, she seemed to suggest, at least to him, that the two of them might go off on their own wherever they liked.

The three of them had a wonderful time that night, wandering among the stalls, strolling over to a chestnut grove, joining some people they knew from the city, dancing together with the peasants in front of the church, chewing their way through some tasteless cakes, until their eyelids grew heavy and they went back to the barn to sleep. They simply could not stop laughing over all they had done and all they had seen—the toys they had bought, the loving couples they had disturbed, the game of cards—they laughed about everything, everything that had happened that night early in autumn. And they went on laughing until finally the time came to decide, in the same spirit of lightheartedness, where they would sleep.

They were wakened at dawn by the beating of drums in the early morning chill. They lit a fire in the courtyard and managed to warm themselves, though not so much from standing in front of the pitiful fire as from running to and fro in search of dry wood. The morning, like the previous night, sped by unnoticed. Pleasantly tired by their revels and sorry that the festivities had passed so quickly, they gathered their things and set off when the sun was just past its zenith.

*   *   *   *

The purple of an early evening stained the slopes of the hills and dappled their faces with shadow. An indefinable sorrow spread like a hidden sigh through the still warm air and left a weary drowsiness which could not be dispelled even by the playful trilling of the mountain swallows soaring away into the deep blue vault of the evening sky. And everything—the trilling, the gentleness of the slowly dying day, the winged cloud on top of the hill—everything was powerless to take its last farewell. Even the gentle rustling of the parched grass seemed to be yearning for some kind of parting word and begging for pity. Everything, everything somehow vaguely reminded him of a holiday that had passed, that still lingered in his spirit but had become no more than a shadow, a light that had died.

He felt all this vaguely, hazily, as though it were no more than a distant whisper. Unconsciously, as if in a trance, as if rocked gently by the waves of some inaccessible distant thought, he walked down the track as though he were not wandering through hills but straying distractedly back down those misty paths he had followed in the past and on which his earlier days had left their faint half-frozen track, unclear in the first snowfall of the year.

This whispering he heard; was it the rustling of the first yellow leaves, which he could not yet see, or was it the song of the mountain swallows preparing for their journey south? The swallows had come long ago, and the spring of his life had long since passed, leaving only the bitter taste of yearning, the longing for the breath of spring, for laughter and flowers. He could not tell if this was a wish or a longing for something he could not remember, a sense of regret for something, whatever it may have been (if it had indeed been), which had passed unfelt but lingered on unfulfilled in his desires—walks in the hills or through the wide fields when waves of recollection flood through one free and unchecked, evenings with friends over a glass full of the warmth of sincere confessions that leave no trace of shame, the sound of a guitar on nights flooded with moonlight. But there was only this sense of sorrow for something real in the tear-drops of rain which harden in the soul—only that, and nothing else.

But the holiday of his spring had passed unfelt. It had not even left a mark on the memory. Now there were the first flecks of hoarfrost on his hair. His spring had slipped past so smoothly that he could not be sure that it had ever been a part of his life. Perhaps it was only a pretty tale that people told, a story from a book. But no, it really had been and was gone. That was the way it had to be. After all, he knew people—or so he believed—who had spent this holiday of spring differently. But he, he . . . he could think of nothing. And why? He simply could not remember when and where he had gone wrong. He had never even experienced a true orgy of sensuality—thrusting bodies seized by fierce, blinding spasms. So far he had never met a woman who had not become a spinster. Those sessions over a glass had always turned into filthy dawns after which, in the stuffy vapors of a hangover, he could not clearly remember with whom he had been drinking or what he had drunk. His few chance acquaintances were only fellow-travelers whom he tolerated and who helped him to kill his time. He had never truly loved, nor had anybody truly loved him, he had never sacrificed and could not remember anybody ever holding out a helping hand to him when all was crumbling around him, when he no longer knew which way to turn.

The swallows were leaving. . . . But this hellish thirst remained unquenched. And yet his teeth were still tightly clenched. He seemed to be hoping that one day the great

bells would ring out in him as well for that holiday of which
he had been dreaming in the desolation of his loneliness.

It was then that something happened which none of them
had expected, not even he, something which one no longer
dreams of, which one never believes will come. It marked
the end of all the expectations of holiday. Summer leaves
with the swallows, as everyone knows. They turned down
a side road and crossed a deserted heath covered with a
tangle of blackberry bushes. He was already on the point
of apologizing to them for leading them down this overgrown track when their cries of delight stopped him short.

They were standing on tiptoe in the purple of the evening, stretching up through the prickly branches to reach the
berries at the top, heedless of the scratches. They crammed
their mouths with the bittersweet berries until their faces
were smeared all over with the dark blood of the fruit. They
were carried away by the pleasure. He found himself standing closer to the younger sister. As he picked the berries he
caught himself, almost involuntarily, looking back to her,
again and again. She was drenched in the deep gold of the
setting sun, and he could see a blue hungry kiss, like a stain,
upon her knee, whenever her skirt was lifted by a branch.
It was only then that he noticed the beauty of her body.
He had watched her before, when they went bathing in the
river. There on the riverbank, she had not seemed at all attractive beside her sister's ripe figure. But now for some
reason—perhaps because of her smile and her wholehearted
delight in the fruitpicking—he was overwhelmed by a longing, tearful to the point of pain, for the holiday he had never
enjoyed, a longing which tore at his very insides and left
him weak and dazed. He realized that never in his life had
he had a companion who was in the full bloom of her youth,
never had he felt the light caress of ringing laughter and
broken cries. Never had he been able to sigh, "Ah! what a
girl." Never had he been able to love spontaneously, without the usual affectations that silted up his life.

Suddenly she gave a frightened cry. He was standing

beside her at that moment. He was afraid she had stepped on a snake. She stared at him, pale, her eyes filling with tears. Then he remembered the little yellow wasps in summer—the thin, striped bodies with their long, protruding stings—and now he caught sight of one. There was a tiny spot on her hand that was already beginning to swell into a bump under a red spot of blood. Almost without thinking he caught her little hand, red with blood and fire of sunset, and began to suck the swelling. He did so because he knew that this was the best way of reducing it. She allowed him to do so without any resistance and watched him carefully with calm eyes full of a soft trust.

He held her hand to his lips—for no more than an instant, it seemed to him. Then he felt as though a fever had seized him. Something was happening between them as she gazed at his head bent upon her. She sensed that this feeling of pleasure which flooded her like the ruddy flush of evening was not simply a feeling of relief. It was, she realized, like a first kiss. Gently, like the falling dusk, unhurriedly, with even a suggestion of regret, she drew back her hand. This sombre man, whose relationship with her sister she had never questioned, this man who had seemed so distant, so far above her that she could never reach to him, whose very presence had forced her to go on thinking of herself as a child, this man who, she believed, had never noticed her, was now desiring her. And she had always thought that she had nothing in herself to offer, that she alone was of no value in his eyes or in the eyes of others.

He spun around, almost a full circle, as though caught. "It's nothing. She's not hurt. The swelling will go down now in a few moments." He was speaking to her sister, and now he walked over to her. She fixed him with a questioning look, uncertain of what to make of her younger sister's frightened appearance. She was not, as he discerned immediately, either mocking or reproachful.

The twilight died away, leaving the dark body of the early evening. The shadows of the hills slipped down into its

embrace. Over in the east a star was shining. A yellow
leaf floated to the ground in a stray wind.

"It's autumn," he thought sadly. "The swallows are leaving. And when they have gone, blankets of fog will cover
our dreams. Then the lonely can find companions only in
the rain. And I—will I go on forever, pursuing the song of
the swallows?" He approached her silently and took her
arm, but she pushed him away with her elbow. She nodded
in the direction of the younger sister who was keeping pace
with them.

"So what!" he exclaimed aloud, "I'm her brother-in-law,
aren't I? We'll be married this time next week!"

She stopped dead. She had expected anything, anything,
just not this. In fact, his confusion had distracted her. She
had been expecting quite the opposite, because it seemed to
her that nothing had escaped her notice—not that there
had been anything significant to notice. Or was it simply
that she was not capable of noticing anything really significant?

ŽIVKO ČINGO

Argil's Decoration

Paskelia is surely the loveliest spot in our valley, but, to be quite honest, it's no setting for a story. It's so far away from the rest of the world that you have to travel a good many miles, even from the nearest road, before you hit the village. And now even the village has vanished. "Paskelia, my son, has gone to the devil," said old Noer Levkovski. "Our Paskelia's dead, dear child. Poor Paskelia. Ah, and what strapping young men were born there. Men and women such as only the Good Lord Himself could have wished for. Those were people, real people. Ah well, God rest their souls—our neighbors the Devievs, uncle Nazer and Laster Tricheski—they were grand folk, indeed they were. And old Daddy From—what about him? He was a musician if ever I knew one. I swear you couldn't find such a fine piper even if you traveled a long way from this valley of ours. A musician, you say—that's nothing—even if he is a piper. Ah, but there was more to him than that, you can take my word for it. Heaven help me if I lie. Old Daddy From could wring the heart out of a stone with his playing. Ah well, he's also gone."

They've all gone, all gone from Paskelia. By now the

Živko Čingo is probably the most widely translated and most frequently anthologized of the new generation of Macedonian short story writers. He was born in 1936 in Velgošti, a village on Lake Ohrid near Struga, a cultivated town in a region rich in Macedonian history where the founders of the Macedonian literary consciousness, the brothers Miladinov, lived in the middle of the nineteenth century. Čingo, a graduate of the university at Skopje, has to date produced two collections of stories, *Paskelia* (1963) and *New Paskelia* (1965), and both have been greeted ecstatically by Macedonian reviewers and critics. His novel, *Golem's Water* (1970), was also received with enthusiasm.

woods have surely grown up all around. Perhaps the birds
have come down from the hills and made their homes in the
warm nests built by men. Perhaps the vineyards of Paskelia
have dried out, for vines are like people. They soon wither
if you leave them. And the vineyard cottages upon the hill
are surely deserted now. That was where the richest valley
lay, right below the cottages. In spring, of course, it was
covered in green. That's just what I wanted to tell you
about. It was spring then, and the whole valley was green.
Well, no, perhaps it wasn't really all green, but, believe me,
the leaves reached up till they brushed the sky and set it
quivering with green. Then everything round about was
flushed with this golden green of the sun and the leaves.
Perhaps it wasn't all really like that, you understand, but
what the hell—that's how it seemed to me then. I was in
love. Yes, you see, even in those days one could fall in love.
One could fall in love and not care a damn about time.
And I fell head over heels in love. I was completely done
for, my friends. Ah, that was love—hellish love. I fell for
the farm bailiff's daughter, Itrina Isailovska. We must have
been struck by a thunderbolt, both of us together. What an
awful time for that to happen.

In those days time did not seem to exist at all. Every spare
second was swallowed up by meetings. And each brief moment stolen from the day passed in a flash. We would
scramble up to the vineyards, wary as rabbits because it was
still dusk and someone might see us. Then we would sit
down on the ground, and no sooner had we done so than it
would be time for the evening meeting. All around us young
men and girls would be calling to each other, singing some
new work-song. My little brother was always whistling and
calling to me in his trembling voice. That voice of his, that
damn whistling! I came pretty close to hating my younger
brother. His cursed whistling and Itrina Isailovska's voice.
It was like living in flames.

"Are you going, my angel?" Itrina would whisper softly
under her breath.

Ah, that voice of hers, my friends. I've never heard such a voice. It was like the river glinting down in the valley, molten and glowing in the evening sun—my dear Itrina's voice. "Are you going?" she would whisper. "Are you going, my gentle colt?" she would ask breathlessly, lying among the leafy vines. Oh Lord, Lord, the earth was hot, so hot it almost scorched you. The flames were so fierce you couldn't open your eyes. Everything was topsy-turvy. Only Itrina's voice was clear, steady, insistent.

"Why are you going, my dearest?" she asked. "For God's sake! Am I no good?"

"Don't go on so, Itrina," I mumbled. "Don't go on so. You're really hurting me. This is something you don't understand. I have to go."

"It's terrible," she said, taking the white flowers from her mouth and slowly buttoning her blouse with one hand. "Terrible, terrible," she whispered. "I'm thoroughly corrupt, Argil Petronievsky, I'm a damned woman. Nobody loves me. I'm a devil, I tell you. Everybody runs away from me."

"No, no," I said, to console her, and I bent over her wide brow. And any man who bent over Itrina would be a poor fish if he didn't fall for her completely. With her you simply lost your head, melted away.

"Hey Argil! The Secretary's come, the Secretary, Comrade Leunko," the sound of my younger brother's frightened voice reached us. "Hurry you fool! Hurry, the Secretary's here."

Oh, for Christ's sake, the Secretary, I thought, and heavy drops of sweat broke out all over my body. Cold tremors shot through my veins. The Secretary! Ah yes, of course, Comrade Secretary! A haze came before my eyes, I remember, and I began to see terrible scenes. No matter what you were thinking of, no matter where you were looking, he was here, there, and everywhere—Comrade Secretary. Comrade Leunko with his puffy, unshaven face, his nose straight and serious. But this, of course, was not important. His eyes were deep and dark. Comrade Secretary had doubtless slept very little, there could be no denying it. His gaze was sharp as a sword. He would have sliced his way through everything that lay before him. His gaze was like a sword of steel. And his voice loud, clear, and remorseless.

"Hmm, let's get a few things straight, comrades. I want to hear more of the reports on sectors one, five, eight, and thirteen. We must make a thorough analysis. Under the item 'other matters' on the agenda, comrades, let's consider the matter of the bailiff's donkey in the collective's wheat fields —gross negligence. We must be self-critical," the Secretary insisted and then became as silent as the grave, passing his cold gaze from one face to another, staring sharply with his small slant eyes. You had the impression that he knew everything and that nothing could be hidden from this monster.

"We must be self-critical." My jawbone moved but the words just wouldn't come out. I wanted to tell them straight away about everything, but you just needed to meet that glance, my friends, that fearful glance, and all sensible thoughts fled from your mind. Everything became jumbled and tumbled in your mind. You couldn't make head nor tail of anything. How did all this happen?

It happened during the great holidays. It was my duty, as a young man, to keep watch in the church and note who went there. This was to help us find out how many people were really committed to Party ideology. I carefully observed everybody who came, and I cursed every one of them most fiercely in my soul. They all hid their eyes from me. Yes, traitors' faces are not serene. Even God Himself seemed to be in a tight corner. Just let Him try to argue about religion, I thought. Just let Him try, if he has the nerve, and I turned my head proudly to take a good look around the church. But she, Itrina, damn her, pretended to know nothing of all this; I looked once at her and she looked back three times. I frowned, and she smiled, so gently, so warmly, looking me straight in the eyes. Ruin.

She even wagged her finger at me as she came over to where I was standing. Utter ruin, I thought, and drew back into a dark corner of the church. My instructions all deserted me, and I begged the saints, whispering as softly as I could, to save me from this fiend of a girl. But she only went on smiling, so warmly, so gently, with her sparkling eyes. "No, Itrina, no," I whispered. "You're the bailiff's daughter. Our ways are quite different. They will never meet. It's all over with your class, you scum, you killers." And yet it was so pleasant for me to go on looking into those light green eyes. My hands began twitching, first one, then the other. I knew that they longed to touch her thick fair hair, which smelt of sunflower seeds. I even thought of trying to nibble her hair. Ah, my dear friends, can one really nibble hair? But you know that even that is possible. What was to be done?

"So then, Argil," her voice cut in on my thoughts, "you too have begun to believe in God."

"You know, Comrade . . .," I said, and then coughed to cover up the word, to show that I had made a mistake, that she was no comrade of ours and did not deserve to be addressed this way. Choosing my words with great care, I told her pompously: "You, Itrina Isailovska, have nothing to discuss with me. It is no concern of yours if I happen to be in the church. A man is always free to change his mind in this life."

"Oh, yes," she said. "A man does sometimes change his mind. A man really does sometimes change his mind in this life," she went on, holding her hand to her mouth but barely hiding the merriment she struggled to contain.

She was a fox, a cunning little fox. But I was equal to her little game. The Secretary had stuffed me full of good advice on how to handle this matter. I knew by heart what I had to say to her. Everything—word for word. The Lord God is a counterrevolutionary and a robber of the people. The Lord God is a scrounger and a plunderer. Down with private property, down with the gentry. Ah, I knew it all

perfectly, although I must admit that my heart missed a
beat or two as I spoke these words.

"Why don't you pray like other people, Argil?" asked
Itrina, winking at me.

"I do it my own way," I mumbled, for the question had
caught me off guard. I clearly hadn't been prepared for
such a question.

"I know your way," said Itrina, and as she spoke she
crept up, quiet as a cat. "I know what you want here."
Itrina was a strange girl. She had such warm breath and
burning breasts. Lord forgive me.

"I know, my angel," Itrina whispered, her voice ablaze.
"I know everything."

"Ah, Itrina Isailovska," I mumbled, hunching my shoulders, and called on all the saints in my most supplicating
voice to save me from this fiendish girl. "Dear Lord, Saint
Petko, Mary the Virgin Mother, Saint Peter, and good Saint
Clement, save me from the bailiff's daughter. Amen." But
the saints seemed bent on revenge. Not one of them so much
as blinked an eye. What could a man do, having nowhere
else to turn, but fall upon her ample bosom?

So, my good friends, that's how it began. I wished myself
dead at once. I had deceived my comrades, I had become a
Judas. My name was damned as a traitor to the Party. But
how was I to explain all this, how would I be able to hold
up my head and look the Secretary straight in the eye?

"We must be self-critical, we must be self-critical." All I
seemed to hear was this voice, heavy as lead, coming at me
from all sides. This voice was beating on my forehead,
beating on my head, beating me everywhere, and tearing at
the roots of my being.

One day—skin me alive if I wasn't truly self-critical that
day! Ah, that was self-criticism! The girls were all crying
their hearts out and my comrades gave me fiery words of
encouragement. I was embraced and congratulated by
everyone.

"Victory is ours, victory is ours! Victory is ours!" they

shouted. And for the first time that same day Traiche Petlevski opened his mouth and told us in a voice full of emotion: "I, comrades, Traiche Petlevski, recommend with all my heart that our dear Comrade Argil should be awarded a decoration. A decoration, comrades!" he said, bursting into loud sobs. Oh, that was happiness, that was life, those were comrades!

"Are you getting on all right now?" Itrina asked once, upon meeting me. "How have you been, Comrade Argil?"

"Fine, fine," I answered, holding my head high as I walked past her without stopping. My footsteps rapped on the ground, and my decoration clinked importantly on my chest.

"Wait," Itrina called to me in a husky voice. "Have you confessed everything?" she asked, and bit her lip. "Have you, Argil? Have you confessed everything?"

"Yes, Itrina Isailovska," I answered, changing my tone. "I have told everything, and now, I admit, my soul is much lighter. Now I feel like a man. My soul is singing."

"Your soul is lighter," said Itrina, and drops of blood seemed to trickle from her mouth. "Lighter, huh? Pah!" she exclaimed and began scratching her face. "Pah! you bloody devil!" She folded her arms over her breasts. "Pah! What a goddamned fool I was," she cried with a loud sob. "How could I have let you lay a finger on me! You . . . pah! I'll kill myself, I swear I will!" Itrina broke away and ran through the vineyards like one possessed, breaking the young flowering creepers, falling headlong. Then she struggled to her feet, laughing, and shouted, "Look here," she lifted her dress as she spoke, revealing her lovely strong legs. "Look here," she repeated, stroking her thighs. "Now I'm going off to the soldiers, to lie with them on their great-coats. I'll lie with them, by God, I will."

Itrina began sobbing uncontrollably and then set off slowly, clumsily down toward the valley. She walked, bent close to the ground, as if wounded in the side. She looked as if she might collapse on the spot at any moment. But she went, and she never again returned to our valley.

This happened at dusk, when people were already calling one another to the evening meeting. I walked furtively along the most distant track to avoid meeting any of my comrades. I was afraid, perhaps, that they might hear that I too was crying.

"What's all this? Talking aloud to yourself?" asked the Secretary, appearing from nowhere and pursing his thin, dark lips.

"It's a . . .," I stammered. "It's a song that's been running in my mind, Comrade Secretary. A song about self-criticism. I'm overflowing with feeling—that's why I want to write the song," I explained, quickly brushing away my tears.

"Ah yes," said the Secretary openly. "That's a fine thing, a song about self-criticism," he repeated, scratching his head. "Yes, that would really be wonderful . . . a song about self-criticism."

Then he gave me a strong, comradely embrace and, holding ourselves erect, we set off for the evening's meeting. The whole way we sang a song of victory.

DIMITAR SOLEV

The Round Trip of a Shadow

All through the long, hot summer afternoon the man tramped along the dusty, deserted streets. He was walking right across the town, from one end to the other. He was wearing a railwayman's coat, but none of the municipal buses would stop for him, for, slung over his shoulder, like a saddle made to measure, was a coarsely woven sack filled with dirt, and protruding from its neatly fastened top, as if from the neck of a flower-pot, was a young tree with soft bark and a pliant stem, which hung down like a tiny cascade over the man's bowed head.

Krume the railway worker, father of four boys, was retired now, and he no longer carried the railwayman's flashlight in his hand or wore stiff boots on his feet. The few remaining strands of hair on his head, relieved of the pressure of his peaked cap and exposed to all winds, real and unreal, danced in the air like broken threads of cobweb. His soft pockets were full of crisp permits issued by the Town Council and addressed to a firm of undertakers. The old railwayman carried his burden with placid resignation, as though it had grown from his back, and, although the melting midday sun beat down on him, he trudged on, unperturbed by any thought of the great distance that separated one end of town from the other.

Dimitar Solev was born (1930) and educated in Skopje, the city in which this story is set, and has lived most of his life there. After his graduation from the University of Skopje in 1955, Solev entered the journalistic profession. He has since had an important place in the city's literary life. He has edited several literary magazines, has published four volumes of short stories, and has written for television and radio. Solev is a prominent Macedonian literary critic, but it is his novel, *The Short Spring of Mone Somonikov* (1964), which has established his reputation among his countrymen.

The graveyard was always at the far end of the town. The more the town expanded, the farther away the grave-yard was moved. The living did not wish to have the dead on their doorsteps. The new city dwellers were just like old villagers, concerned only for their own peace and quiet, so they kept moving the graveyard to the edge of town; they had little regard for its residents' eternal rest.

When Krume had buried Mitrush it had been summer, and in summer the bramble bushes were dusty and covered with violet burrs; then the graveyard had been at Crno Pole, at the south end of town. "It's not a good place to be buried," Krume the railwayman had muttered to the mortal remains of his son Mitrush. The war was still going on then, and the graves were very much like the entrench-ments; indeed, each could swallow a man. The graveyard served both the Christians and the Jews, and its dark earth was always deeply rutted with cart tracks. Below the grave-yard was the railway station with its sidings, above it stood Mount Vodno with its isolated villas. When he had climbed Crno Pole and had left behind him the coal smoke and the smell of slag, the railwayman had wiped his eyes, clearing them not so much of the mists of Vodno as of his own salt tears. But when he had arrived on the flat ground of the graveyard, riddled with mole burrows, there had been the scent of uprooted flowers, of melted wax, of overturned earth, of dried leaves. Krume the railwayman had planted a young tree on Mitrush's grave. His son had died in sum-mer, and Krume thought that he should have proper shade. All around, jutting out knee-high from the ground above the graves of the rich Jews and Christians, he had seen the marble gravestones, those cool counters of hot loss. Krume the railwayman had taken to drinking his brandy up here on Saturday evenings. His soft cap, with the sweaty inside turned up toward the darkening sky, would lie in his lap like a fallen bird.

When the war was ended, however, they had moved the graveyard to the east end of the city, to Usje. Behind the stone quarry, beneath the yellow slopes of the vineyard, the graveyard was now placed in another site, on a stretch of coarse, sandy ground. The new cement factory showered its fine dust over the graves, while from behind the nearest hill the silence was continually shattered by ragged bursts of rifle fire from the military camp. The residents of the new graveyard, elbowed out of the way by the hurly-burly of the city, still failed to find peace. From the field on which the graves were springing up like molehills one could even see in the distance a tidy belt of soft green—the airport. And though it seemed highly improbable, the roar of the tiny airplanes taking off could often be heard.

When Krume the railwayman moved the grave of his son Mitrush there, he was not able to bring along the young tree which shaded the grave. So the little tree was left to spread the shade of its new branches over the mound of earth that used to fill the grave, and there it remained until the bulldozers came to level the old graveyard and to prepare the site for the new buildings. But there was not a single young tree in the new graveyard; the soil was dry and gray. So Krume had gone to the nursery, had chosen a new tree, and had carried it over his shoulder to the graveyard by the stone quarry. Mitrush died in summer, he thought to himself, and he must have proper shade.

The new tree had a soft bark, and the stem was pliant near the top. As he was treading down the earth round the roots, he felt the shoot sinking deeper and deeper into the soil. Krume then watered it, and afterward he used to come every Saturday as dusk was falling to see if it had taken root and was giving shade. The red bus would come from the town, leaving behind it a long tail of gray dust. At the last stop it would shake out a few women dressed in black. These women would scrabble the sign of the cross with their dry hands as they scattered out through the graveyard. Then they would untie their black scarves, let down their hair, and begin their mourning. At this point Krume the railwayman would get up from under his tree and steal away, for the women's whining crawled like a caterpillar up his spine. But once again, as before, Krume had seen the tree slowly take to the dead earth and begin to put out the stunted leaves, which soon turned white with dust from the cement factory. It even threw a skimpy shadow, which gave some shade to the roots (although very little to the mound of the grave). During each visit, after he had drunk his brandy, Krume the railwayman would fill the bottle with water and sprinkle the roots of the tree. So it was that this tree also took root and cast its shadow, at least over the head of Mitrush's second grave.

But soon the graveyard was moved again, this time to the north end of the town, to Butel. As had happened on the previous occasion, the tree had grown and flourished, and Krume could not dream of moving it from one end of town to the other. After having transferred Mitrush's mortal remains, already once disturbed in the first resettlement, Krume had continued for some time to visit the graveyard by the quarry until he saw that the young tree had not simply turned white or dried out but had been torn out by the roots like a clump of knotgrass. At the end, the old graveyard, with its uprooted trees and vacant graves, looked like a field of ruined molehills; it seemed that the bones had been snatched up for flight. Krume the railwayman could not bear to watch the bulldozers flattening this ground, which had by now already been dug and redug; he could not stand their smoothing over the surface as though nothing had ever happened, as though nothing had ever been there.

So he had left behind him not only the wailing of the women but also the sounds of the machines. After his last visit, Krume the railwayman had caught the bus—now that it was empty it had been easy for him to get on. He stuck his ticket to his lower lip and chose a seat close to the driver. The seat seemed familiar to him, for Krume, during his long years of service on the railways, had always worked as an engine stoker. Rain began to fall from the darkening sky. The bus made its way to the city with raindrops spattering its windows. At each stop more and more mud was tramped in by the passengers. The fresh scent of rain rose from their steaming shoulders. The mist was thick on the inside of the windows, and the floor by the exit door was littered with an ever-increasing pile of used tickets. Thus they came to the town. Seen through the windows, the glistening streets looked like flooded rivers at high-water mark. It was only when he stepped down at his stop that Krume noticed a carnation lying squashed on the floor in the sodden mess of mud and used tickets.

Krume made his way homewards, stepping round those puddles he managed to see in time. He had spat out the pulpy ticket that was sticking to his lip, but he could not drive from his mind the thought that now a new tree should be planted on Mitrush's latest grave at Butel. With this worry on his mind, a worry for the morrow, he closed the gate behind him and stared at the lighted kitchen window. His old and ailing wife had been waiting for him so they could drink their tea together and exchange a sigh before he retired to bed, where they lay together, back to back.

Many years had passed and many different times had come and gone since the death of Mitrush, their first-born son and (so far) the only child they had lost. Their other sons, thanks to the times, had found their feet—found their feet and taken to their heels. No sooner would one of them grow up than he would vanish from their midst. They had all learned some trade or other and then had jumped into patent-leather shoes to follow the swish of a skirt. As time passed, letters would arrive, but their sons had never returned. Old Krume and his wife, accompanying the postman to the gate, had watched their wickerwork fence getting thinner every day.

Nothing was left of the fields any more—all the meadows with their grass, brambles, earth, and stones, had been swallowed up by the buildings: the Art School, the Kindergarten, the local Polyclinic, apartment blocks. The dry, yellow paths that had run like rivulets through the meadows were now almost as wide as the streets. Above the little houses the skyscraper apartments with their colored balconies towered like tall poplars, and day and night new sounds poured down from them. People were digging the ground from under their feet in order to climb up on top of each other's heads.

But Krume the railwayman had stayed close to the earth and had waited until the day when they would move him out as well, although his own little house could hardly be seen above ground. The higher the buildings rose above them, the lower Krume bent his head. Did his old age fit in with the youthfulness of the town? The old railwayman gave no thought to this question; he simply prayed, lifting his head toward the all-comforting sky, that his house would not be swept from the face of the earth before he himself and his old wife were gone.

Everywhere the old buildings were being torn down; they had to tear down everything before they began building again. Krume understood this and often explained it to his aged wife. Patiently, as if talking to a deaf person, he would explain to her that first the old had to be torn down before the new could be built. And even if the new buildings were not begun at once, the old ones still had to be torn down because they were an eyesore beside the already existing new constructions. "Must we go too?" she would ask, looking up at the roof, which leaked whenever it rained hard. "Yes," answered the old railwayman Krume, but he would add a silent prayer, "Only let it be as late as possible. They'll tear down our place, that's for sure. But if only they'll do it after we've gone." "And the graveyard too?" the old woman would ask again, her eyes already half closed. "That too," the old railwayman would reply. "If the dead won't make way for the living, who will?" His old wife lay in the bed, wondering all the time whether she would live to see the dawn lighting her window the next day. "One must die," she would murmur to herself, as if for consolation, before going to sleep. "One must die, old man." "One must die," the old man would whisper in agreement before turning on his side so they were lying back to back. "One must die, old man, but God send us health while we're living."

One day, early in the morning, the old railwayman had eased his sticky back from the hot sheets and climbed up onto the roof to replace the tiles. From above, as from a dovecote, he watched his wife hanging out the washing to dry on an iron pole, one patch next to another, one spot next to another. That iron pole had once been used by their sons as a horizontal bar, and no matter how much she implored them, she had never succeeded in recovering it for drying the washing, not until they had grown up. There was a time when their sons had hung like monkeys from that iron bar, which now flecked the clean clothes with rust. That was, of course, before they came down to earth, poor things. And now that they had come down to earth, they had gone for good. The winds of life had scattered them. No sooner had they set foot on the ground than the wind had whirled them away. No doubt they had grown strong enough to tackle other bars. The old railwayman fixed the tiles against the rains to come and, without calling down to his wife at all, watched her stretching up toward the rusty bar. The older we grow, the smaller we become, he reflected as he came down from the roof. Then he washed his hands at the pump, which had been wheezing for a good many years, and his wife put a light vegetable stew on the fire.

Now that none of the boys were any longer with them, Krume would always tell his wife where he was going whenever he left the house. "I'm off," he would say, "to see what's going to happen to our house. Maybe they're going to pull it down"; or he might tell her, "I'm going to have a look at Mitrush's grave." The old woman, long since incapable of leaving the house, agreed to everything, so long as she knew where he was going. She did not really need to know, but his telling her seemed to be some kind of assurance that he would return. "All the children took after you," she would grumble to him whenever she knew he would not be going out again that day. "Not one of them ever came back, and you were just the same, always a wanderer." The old railwayman, sitting outside in the yard, would fiddle impatiently with his cap and give a light, dry cough. He knew she was right, and although he was conscious of his power over her, he felt his own impotence when faced with her recriminations. So he would do his best to conciliate her before going out the next time. His conciliation usually took the form of entrusting her with the task of making the stew as juicy as possible; this was an unspoken guarantee that he would return.

Anyway, where else could this old railwayman have stayed without any of his sons to support him? He would wander around the town, he would follow again one of the few real remaining interests in his life, and then he would go back home, relieved to know that from one day to another his worries would grow no greater. The only thing left him, the only remaining pleasure out of all he had had, was his flask of brandy. It used to be a whole bottle while he was still working, but now that he was retired it had been reduced to a flask. His neighbor, God bless him, was still sprightly enough to run a small distillery at home, and Krume, as soon as he went into retirement, had made an advance payment to the man for a flask of brandy every other evening. Despite his wife's opposition, he had succeeded in convincing her that one flask every other evening was not only better for him but also came to less than a whole liter every Saturday evening. And so every evening he would first put his feet up a little after strolling around the town, and then he would have a quiet drink on the kitchen doorstep, looking out at the buildings soaring like poplars all around them.

However, although it was these same concrete poplars surrounding them on all sides which threatened to drive him and his wife out of their little house and perhaps deeper and deeper into the ground, Krume the railwayman would return home with the firm feeling that it was on this doorstep that he would find peace—or at least in the half-empty flask. Indeed, although his gadding around town seemed to his wife to be pure indulgence, Krume was finding these trips more and more disillusioning. The clerks in the various offices he visited were each time noticeably less willing to listen to him, and his comrades on the park benches were becoming more and more tedious. Besides, the streets seemed longer and longer to his tired feet.

Nevertheless, Krume the railwayman was gradually becoming convinced that before long he would win his case and earn the right to retain the present location of his house and that before long he would find a better location for Mitrush's grave. If he succeeded, it would be more the result of his persistence than of the strength of his claim. The officials behind their counters issued him documents as though they were handing him his own death certificate; they hoped, no doubt, that this would be the last that they would be seeing of him. But the old railwayman was unperturbed by their air of indifference; what mattered to him was only that something in him should be kept alive. How could this be managed unless he took care of things long dead?

Mitrush was dead. The other sons were also dead, in another way; the house would die—sooner or later. Everything was dead. This would all be quite clear to Krume when he was away from home. But it was quite a different matter when he was back home again. Then his old wife spoke about all these things as though they were living. Could one really think of all these things as dead when one still wanted so to live? The town did not wish to rub shoulders with the cemetery, the living did not want to be close to the dead, yet Krume the railwayman and his old wife quite unconsciously lived with these dead things as though they were living.

"Have you been to see Mitrush?" the old woman would

ask when her husband came back from town. "Yes," Krume
would answer, as though he had been with somebody with
whom he had spoken only a few minutes earlier. "How is
he?" the old woman would ask, her voice quivering with
the hope that he would not be worse than the day before.
"He's fine," the old man would answer. "He ought to find
it better in the new graveyard." "Did you plant the tree?"
the old woman would ask, for the more her own movements became restricted the more she knew about his. "I
didn't get around to it today," the old man would frown
to himself, "but I'll see to it tomorrow." "We must hurry,"
she would respond, "so that our poor Mitrush at least has
some shade for his head." "He will, my dear," Krume would
say to comfort her. "They couldn't manage it today, but
everything'll be ready tomorrow. That's what they told me;
that's what they promised me." "Poor Mitrush," whispered
the old woman, no longer listening to him. "If only he had
a shade above his head so he might rest at last."

And she herself began to find greater peace of soul as
her wasted body grew more and more still. The old railwayman would listen to her at night, shifting in bed, struggling against strange thoughts. After a while she would
get up, groaning, and walk barefoot over to the wardrobe.
There, in the dark, she would lay out the funeral clothes
and talk to the children. Krume did not have the heart to
interrupt her, and, indeed, he could see no point in doing
so. For she was a somnambulist, sinking deeper and deeper
into her own world. The less she was able to work, the
more she sank into this world of her own. Her world
had been a world of housework; looking after children had
left no time to think about the dead. But since her children,
one by one, had gone their ways, each day seemed itself a
loss and left the house emptier than ever. She herself was
empty-handed; she had no more work and no more cares.
"If only I still had one child left," she would sigh, not
knowing what to do with her hands, "just one child, or
even a grandchild."

Now, when the first pale rays of dawn streaked their windows, they no longer got out of bed as before. Now they would turn their backs to each other and pretend to be still asleep, for why get out of bed when there was nothing waiting to be done? A cup of tea, thin vegetable stew, tea again. They, who had been accustomed to working all their lives for others, now felt that they had nothing to do for themselves. And too many of the things they had sought from life had now been taken from their hands.

However, the old man still got up first. He would go to the market, if only to fill the bottom of his basket with cheap vegetables and then return home for his bread-mash with tepid tea or sour milk. His old wife would wait for him to tell her what sort of vegetable stew he wanted for lunch, then she would go off to wash an old jacket or do a little sweeping.

This was how Krume's day would begin; this was how his wandering around the town would start. But then the town spread out like a drop of ink on blotting paper and the graveyard was moved farther and farther away. The retired railwayman relearned the bus routes for the new graveyard; the bus routes themselves were constantly changing.

Even the registry office came to be tucked away in side-street buildings, each older and more dilapidated than the last, so it was a constant struggle just to keep abreast of all the changes. If one missed out on some change, it was a great problem to gather the lost thread, to bring oneself up to date, to fit into the new scheme of things. This was why old Krume, as soon as he heard whisperings among the pensioners on the park benches of some change to come, would immediately start calling on all the offices, asking for confirmation of the rumor. One never knows, he said to himself, one never knows when one's name might be crossed off the list.

With hard confirmations in his soft pockets the old railwayman would set off once more to tramp around the

town. These new papers, it is true, involved further solici-
tation and more waiting, but the departments that issued
them were at least wise enough not to shift their offices
too far away from the center. For they wished to avoid the
fate of the graveyard. So Krume took to the streets again.
First, he had to get a wagon to move his son's remains;
then, he had to find a man to open up the old grave; then,
he had to find a man to prepare the new grave; finally,
he had to find a priest to give his blessing to Mitrush's
mortal remains. All these matters had to be arranged to
occur at the same time, so this already endless transfer of
his bones might be carried out in the most seemly way,
without conspicuousness or delay.

So without saying anything to his old wife, Krume the
railwayman had moved Mitrush's grave once again. But
this time he had dispensed with all the ceremonies. He had
reached the end, not only of his patience, but also of his
money. One evening, after knocking back a whole flask of
brandy to boost his courage, he had secretly gathered Mitrush's bones, packed them into the market bag and, carrying his strange load, had boarded the bus heading for the
other end of town. "Forgive me, Mitrush," he murmured
to the bag, which he was holding on his knees as gingerly
as a cradle with a newborn babe. Never had Krume felt so
guilty before his first-born son, not even when he had sent
him off with shaven head to a foreign army to relieve the
family of the burden of feeding another mouth. That night,
as he placed his son's bones in the new grave, the old
railwayman swore he would never dig them up again, swore
never to move them, never to touch them, never to disturb
them, not even if every dead body in the town was moved
to make way for expansion.

And now, after so many removals, he was carrying a new
tree over his shoulder. The bag containing the roots lay on
his back as if on a well-worn saddle; the old railwayman
recalled that he had carried his sons like this when he had
climbed with them up the slopes of Vodno. The pliant stem

hung down over his head and shook at every step as though an axe were slicing at its tender bark. The shade cast by the top of the tree was so small that it scarcely covered his steaming head, and the noon sun was shining fiercely, melting the empty streets in its savage heat.

Thus the old railwayman walked from one end of town to the other, carrying the young tree for his eldest son's last grave. The streets opened out before him like the dried-out beds of floodstreams, each more unfamiliar and more deserted than the last, and all the municipal buses shut their rubber-rimmed doors in his face. Dusk was falling by the time Krume the ex-railwayman, father of four boys long since grown, planted a tree on the still fresh grave of his son Mitrush, long since dead. His sweat sprinkled the roots, but when he sat down to rest under the pliant stem, "Now you'll have your shade again, my son," he sighed.

Below and beyond him, in a circle around the outskirts of the town, he could just make out the several places the graveyard had been. The sun sank into the ground, burrowing under the city in a haze of bloodshot dust. The railwayman raised his head toward the sky and felt it resting on his back as he stood beside the grave of his son Mitrush.

The Body That Belonged to No One

The strongest man in the village spat into the river, then turned around and looked back.

"It's Lenni!" he shouted; "Lenni's coming!"

Little Lenni, who was still a few hundred yards away, came running full tilt toward the small group of people. When they heard her coming, the people ran to meet her, calling out her name. Only old Mijo was left on the river bank, standing knee-deep in the sand, bent over the body of a young girl that had been cast up by the river early that morning.

The people clustered around Lenni, unable to hold back their questions.

"Lenni!" cried her mother. "Lenni! Where on earth have you been, child?"

"But you know, Mummy," said Lenni, "that the teacher never lets me come down when the weather's bad."

Mile Nedelkovski was born in Prilep in 1933, and devotes all his time to writing—to his poetry, to his short stories, and to his plays. He has published several collections of poems, a novel, and one collection of short stories, *Riders of the Wind* (1967).

The story included here depends to some extent upon the very special awareness the Macedonians have concerning their borders. Yugoslavia is contiguous to seven other nations, and her northern frontiers, shared with four of those nations, are quite relaxed; crossing is a simple affair, especially for the inhabitants of the border towns and villages. But the three frontiers to the south—the frontiers Macedonia shares with Albania, Greece, and Bulgaria—are disputed, relations are bad, and crossing is a serious business indeed. The rigidity of these frontiers has disrupted the lives of the local inhabitants considerably, especially the lives of the people in the border towns. This disruption is an experience known acutely by almost every Macedonian.

"Old Mijo pulled a dead girl out of the river, and we all thought it was you."

"Why?" said Lenni. "I never go swimming by myself."

"Lenni," cried her mother, "Lenni, my child. . . ." The mother drew her daughter close.

"But who was drowned then?" asked one of the women.

"Nobody," said another.

"What d'you mean, nobody?" said the strongest man in the village. "She can't be nobody—unless you want to tell me she's a river spirit."

"It's quite clear," he continued. "The river must have carried her down from the border."

"From behind the border," said Lenni's mother. "Maybe she has a mother back there. We ought to return the body," added Lenni's mother.

"Let's send her back," said the strongest man in the village.

Everybody looked up toward the border and then down at the river. Old Mijo was still on the bank, holding the corpse in his lap and rocking it gently.

"Just as if he were praying," said one woman.

"He's crying," said another.

"Old Mijo's crying," said one of the men. "Mijo's crying."

"Enough," said the strongest man in the village, striding over toward Mijo.

"Mijo!" he called. "Hey, Mijo, that's enough, man! She's not one of our children. The river brought her down from the other side of the border, so we'll have to send her back."

"No," said Mijo. "No!" and he bent over the corpse.

The strongest man in the village caught hold of Mijo's shoulder and tried to drag him away from the body. "Listen, man, we've got to send this girl back where she came from. She's maybe got a mother there who'll be looking for her now." The strongest man in the village spoke gently. "We've got to send this girl back, Mijo."

Once again he tried to drag Mijo away from the body,

but Mijo was too quick for him. He suddenly stood up with the body clasped close, struggling to keep his balance.

"All right," he said through his tears. "We'll send her back to her mother."

"It can't be done just like that," said the strongest man in the village. "We can't all go over there. Just Lenni's mother'll come with us."

"All right," said Lenni's mother. "I'll go with you—but nobody else."

The two men and the woman from the village were stopped by a soldier at the border post.

"Where d'you think you're going?" asked the soldier.

"This drowned girl isn't ours," said Lenni's mother to the soldier. "The river brought her down to us from the other side of the border. We want to take her back."

"Maybe the girl has a mother over there," said the strongest man in the village, "and she'll be looking for her now."

"The girl drowned?" said the soldier. "Drowned in the river? That's a shame." The soldier looked back toward the border and then said, "I don't know . . ., I'd better ask the commander."

He went off to the customs house and returned with the commanding officer and several soldiers. The soldiers stood in front of the people from the village and gazed at the body in Mijo's arms.

"A girl," said one of them.

"Female," said another.

"Who is she?" asked the commanding officer.

"We don't know," said the strongest man in the village. "Mijo pulled her out of the river."

"She's not one of our children, Captain," said Lenni's mother. "She comes from behind the border, and she has a mother there who'll be looking for her. We want to take her back, Captain. You've got children too, Captain."

"All right, all right," said the commanding officer, turning away. "We'll have to discuss it with their men."

The soldiers and the three people from the village walked

toward the opposite border post. The commanding officer told the guard on the other side of the border of the drowned girl and said that they wanted to take her back. The guard eventually agreed to call his commanding officer. The two commanders discussed the problem and then explained to the people from the village why it was impossible for them to take the dead body back across the border. There was no village near the border on the other side, they explained, so the river could not have brought the drowned girl down from there. And even if she had been brought down by the river, the dead body could not be returned, because dead bodies had to be buried where they were found.

"All right!" said the strongest man in the village impatiently. "We'll bury the body."

The two men and the woman went back to the village, back to the river bank. Mijo lowered the body again onto the sand and bent down over it, and the other villagers gathered around.

"Damn fools," said the strongest man in the village, "they don't want to take their own dead."

"Fools," said Lenni's mother, "they don't want her."

"Fools," said the villagers and fell silent.

"What shall we do with the body now?" asked one of the women.

"Let's return it to the river," suggested one man.

"We can't," said the strongest man in the village. "No, we can't do that. She isn't a river spirit. We'll bury her in our graveyard."

"Quite right," said Lenni's mother. "That's where we'll bury her."

"Very well," said Mijo. "Let her be buried there. I'll take her home. Lenni's mother better come and get her ready."

"No, no, that won't do," said the strongest man in the village to the women. "She isn't his daughter, so he shouldn't take her home."

"She is mine," said Mijo. "She's mine. I pulled her out of the river."

Mijo turned to the people gathered around him.

"Listen," said Mijo. "Listen," he said through his tears. "I have never buried anyone in my life. Nobody close to me has ever died. I have nobody. I am not from these parts. You all go to the graveyard while I sit at home. My friends," said Mijo, "I have no grave to tend."

"She can't be yours," said the strongest man in the village. "The river carried her down from behind the border. She is ours—everyone's."

"She's mine," said Mijo. "She's mine. I pulled her out of the river." And Mijo began running away, carrying the dead girl.

The strongest man in the village was the first to catch up with old Mijo. He seized him by the neck and forced him down onto the sand.

"You fool!" shouted the strongest man in the village. "She can't be only yours. The river brought her to us."

Thus he took the body of the drowned girl from the old man and strode off with it toward the village, followed by the others.

"Quite right," said Lenni's mother. "Toma was quite right, you know. The girl can't belong only to Mijo."

Mijo lay, choking with sobs, on the sand of the river bank.

The Final Move

A few moves earlier his young opponent had offered him a draw, but the chess master had refused the offer, not because he had noticed some hidden advantage for himself in the apparent equality of position, but simply because half a point would not get him anywhere. This was his last game in the semifinals, and only if he won it, only if this evening he succeeded in winning a whole point, would he be able to go on to the State Championship finals. There was only this single rung to climb before he reached the top of the ladder.

How crucial this victory was to him! For three years he had been struggling unsuccessfully to break through into the finals. He hardly ever found himself competing against any of the people with whom he had begun his chess career. Some had achieved world fame, while others had taken to writing commentaries on other people's games in the chess columns. Yes, one of them was even present at this match, though only as a judge. Nowadays he found he was always

---

Blaže Koneski is almost universally regarded as the dean of Macedonian writers. Born near Prilep in 1921, Koneski has followed a brilliant academic career as a lexicographer and philologist. He has almost singlehandedly established the importance of Macedonian in the history of the language of the Slavic peoples; he is the author of the dictionary of the Macedonian language and of some forty significant philological studies. He has written *A Grammar of the Macedonian Literary Language* (1952–1954), *A History of the Macedonian Language* (1966), and a number of short stories, first collected in *Vineyard* (1955). Since 1948, when he collected his poems in *Land and Love*, he has been preeminent among Macedonian lyric poets. He is also justly recognized as a literary critic and translator.

He is now Professor of Macedonian Literature at the University of Skopje. He has served as Rector of the University and as President of the Macedonian Academy of Arts and Sciences.

pitting his wits against younger people. Some of them were mere children—schoolboys, cocky, nonchalant, ironical toward him because he could not overcome his inclination to put on a show of importance.

Soon they had left him behind. They soon outstripped him, these representatives of the younger generation.

Although he would never have mentioned this to anyone, there were certain moments when he was filled with absolute horror at his inability to keep pace with them. This feeling of horror was, in fact, an old, deep-rooted sensation, something he had lived through before and which was now being reawakened by a different cause.

As a student he had taken part in a large demonstration against the State. When the police had set upon the demonstrators, he had been among the first to make his escape. But he had been weak and in bad condition, so he had begun to lag farther and farther behind in the mob of fleeing students. He could not recognize the faces that were flying past; he saw only countless feet overtaking him, cutting roughly across in front of him, breaking his pace, and leaving him farther and farther behind. The speed of these people dashing past had affected him; it had stirred horror at the thought that he might swiftly be left behind by the crowd, all alone and utterly vulnerable in his great flight.

He would never, as I said, reveal to anyone how deeply he had suffered from this sense of being left behind. What was generally known about him was self-evident anyway— that he was yearning for a sort of rehabilitation. It was quite natural and understandable. On the past two occasions luck had not been on his side, and he had ended up near the bottom of the ladder ("in the lower house" as it is jokingly called). The chess critics concluded, in terse sentences, that he was unable to recover his old form, that he had begun well but had tired quickly and so spoiled the position he had already gained by not having the strength to stick it out to the end. Their comments were certainly fair; he could not resent any of them. It was something else that hurt him; it was those young men whose mocking glances he could feel boring into his back while he pondered interminably, trying to work his way out of a situation from which there was no escape.

What distressed him even more were the general discussions in the chess publications. No names were mentioned, but it would be suggested, for instance, that the title of Chess Master should not be awarded for life but should be periodically defended under tournament conditions because, it had been observed, there were some masters whose development appeared to stop as soon as they received their title.

He was quite aware of the extent to which this affected him personally. In his imagination he always saw his own name in brackets, together with the names of several of his less fortunate colleagues, as an illustration to such articles. They, perhaps, would take the blow easily, with a smile and a shrug as if to say, "It doesn't matter." But he could not reconcile himself so easily; he suffered because chess for him was not just one interest among several others, a fleeting youthful craze. It was a calling in which all his none-too-modest ambitions were engaged. Success in chess was his dream of success in life.

He had gained the title of Chess Master when he was still a student. But, despite the fact that his record at the faculty had been excellent, he was always putting off his studies from one day to the next, and he had never passed all his law examinations. At that time it was not study but a different field of action that had seemed enticing to him. It was a field that seemed at first sight small and, to the nonenthusiast, cramped—sixty-four black and white squares on a board small enough to carry under your arm. But this field opened the way into a world of miraculous experiences which, like those of the real world, demanded that one should tirelessly struggle to assert one's power. Yet these were not coarse, quotidian demands; they seemed a challenge to engage one's very soul in a noble and lofty strug-

gle. The awareness that all victories in this world are sheer
illusion did not detract from the young master's pleasure
in them. He knew that, if one were to reflect a little, one
would realize that many things which seem more important
in life and upon which serious men expend all their energies
may in the end prove to equally fanciful. He concurred with
the attitude, still insufficiently expounded and even less
generally accepted, that chess is an art and that to serve
this art means experiencing not only the delights but also
the sufferings that are involved in the service of an awak-
ened soul.

However, it must be pointed out that the need for pure
intellectual activity is, to a limited extent, linked with other,
more "real" motives, like the desire for a worldly fame that
would ensure a beautiful, pleasurable, varied life. It was
only natural, then, that that motive should also have affected
our young master as well. The poor student, accustomed
to daily poverty, began to be aware of the blessings available to him in the life of chess. The tournaments were generally held in summer resorts or baths, in surroundings of
surprising beauty, freshness, and pleasantness, abounding
in a certain concentrated richness. It was a life to which
this young chess player was already tentatively beginning
to lay some claim, even though he was aware that these
pleasures could be attained only with other people's back-
ing. In the tournament hall, sitting at his board before the
eyes of the silent spectators, he often imagined himself quite
detached, even from his moves. When he would walk at a
measured pace among the chess tables, examining the positions on the other boards, his expression was that of a
man rapt in thought, of intense concentration. Yet somehow a feeling of self-importance imposed itself upon him of
its own accord, prompting him to glance as if by chance at
the spectators in the hope of catching a suggestion of their
approval of his concentration from their faces.

At the resorts, and especially at the baths, the younger
chess players had enjoyed the attention of the ladies, who

were always eager to encourage talented youth. He could recall several romances from those times, the latest of which
had ended in marriage. It had been a wonderful time! The
confined space of the chess board had revealed to him a
wide path for his life. It had once even led to his going
abroad. Thus he seemed to be on the verge of realizing his
fantasies about world tours and tournaments—those dream-
visits to the *haute monde* of chess, the Brazilian plantation
owners or the fabulously rich maharajas, where there were
ballrooms in which beautiful women, covered only with
diaphanous veils, swayed through the night in dances
around a fountain, their dark eyes blazing and flashing with
fire.

What a mockery life had made of these dreams! Life had
filled him with the highest expectations and then thwarted
him by sapping his vitality so that he could neither realize
his ambitions nor even come within sight of them. Now in
his fortieth year, bent over the silent pieces in a small inland
town, he realized that the true power of his imagination had
lain in its ability to conjure up beautiful visions of the life
that lay ahead of him, not in its creative strength in solving
the problems posed by that silent board with its sixty-four
squares. This awareness gave rise to a sense of disharmony
in his soul. A chasm had appeared, and now he would have
to suffer. He had already bid farewell to the dreams of youth,
yet there still remained one thought to which he could not
reconcile himself. Now he felt more sure that he had built
his life upon a false foundation and that the victory which
had seemed to presage the emergence of an exceptional
talent had been no more than a fluke, a bit of luck that was
never to be repeated.

He had come to this tournament firmly resolved to allay
this suspicion. He had hoped secretly that all was not yet
lost, that he could still recover his old form, that his weakness was only a passing phase. So he had flung himself into
the game with all his energy. Everyone who knew him recognized that this was a battle for rehabilitation, but for him

it was something deeper—a showdown with himself, a new assessment of his life. And now he was confronted with the position that would determine whether he would once again be left behind; now he was again on the very threshold, like a man who has been waiting for a long time in line in front of a box office and watches the last tickets disappear as he approaches the window. Would he gain once again the opportunity to match his strength against those who had started with him but had left him far behind—because they had greater talent, greater luck, or greater staying power?

The master considered his position for a long time. The longer he gazed, the more certain he was that his young partner had in fact been over-hasty in offering him a draw a few moves back. His impatience could be easily understood. At the back of the hall a young girl, dressed in red, was waiting for him. From time to time he had left the table to whisper something to her. No doubt he was persuading her to wait just a little longer; perhaps he was hoping that another beautiful evening would yet not be ruined. Perhaps he really would have been more than satisfied to have called it a draw. The master, who always tried to follow his opponent's train of thought, had first sensed this at the moment when he had refused the younger man's offer, and it had seemed then that in his opponent's impatience lay a hope for his own success. But now, a few moves later, he realized that his hope was futile. The position was by no means favorable to him. Indeed, it was doubtful whether now he would even be able to manage to play to the draw. Now that he was faced with his relentless truth, a quiet sense of resignation began to overtake him.

The number of pieces had been greatly reduced in the queen exchange, and his knight (he was playing black) was hemmed in and reduced to the humble task of being a pawn behind which the king could take shelter from the grave danger on H7. And white's bishop was free to roam. His opponent had space for movement, while he was tied to the spot and threatened on almost all sides. What move

could he now make? The options were uninspiring. All that
was left for him to do was to make the obvious move and
advance the pawn one square to protect the king. But this
would simply buy time. It would not really improve his position at all. The master, resigned to his fate, stretched out
his hand to make the move. But just as he was about to
touch the pawn his eye fell on the opposite side of the board.
He quickly withdrew his hand.

Here indeed was a surprise. Was it really possible that
in the white's pawn position there was hidden an opportunity of which—with a certain adjustment of his own position—he might take advantage? Or was his mind deceiving
him? It would involve a sacrifice of two of his four remaining pawns. Then the white bishop would be left unprotected
in the center of the board. The ultimate advantage in the
position would be realized later when his own free knight
might check the white king. Then the bishop would be his.

The master leaned both elbows on the chess table and began moving his eyes over the pieces like an airplane flying
low over a built-up area. But heavens! What an infinite
number of moves were possible after his taking even the
very first step (in which his first pawn was to be sacrificed)!
How could he follow up all the possibilities, how could he
classify them and then make the correct choices that his
sacrifice should not prove to be only laughable—an ordinary piece of desperate recklessness? And he had so little
time left! As his clock moved he plunged into the task of
weighing the possibilities. He sensed that he was confront-
ing the critical move of his career.

While he was visualizing the possibilities, contemplating
the choices, one of the attendants brought him a letter in a
plain blue envelope. The master only glanced at it. "It's from
Maria," he thought—and left it lying on the edge of the
table. He tried again to focus his entire attention completely
on the problem at hand and to make the best use of his time,
which was rapidly running out. His first analysis of a possible sequence of moves revealed that white could make

good return moves and easily ward off his attack. This discovery unsettled him for a moment, and his thoughts became confused. But he took hold of himself and waited for the cloudy fear to disappear and for the imagined board to swim back into focus within his mind.

Nevertheless, it was still too early to resign himself to his king's defense. There were many other ways of handling the situation. Something whispered to him that among these many ways there was hidden one—only one—that would lead him to victory. He must—he would—find that way. Unluckily he did not come upon it immediately; it seemed as though his former intuition had abandoned him, as though his best move was deliberately hiding from him like a naughty child hiding behind the backs of the other children during school break. "Find me! Find me!" it was taunting him. The master made a fresh effort. He leaned even lower over the table and knitted his brows even more closely together, searching, searching.

But, at the same time, he could feel something cold inside him. A metastasizing apathy was spreading throughout his body. Was the idea that there was a way by which he could save his game only a mirage tantalizing a desperate traveler in a desert? "Where is it, if it exists?" he wondered. "It's impossible that I still cannot see it!" Suddenly he caught himself in the simplest form of self-delusion. He had already retraced his way over several of the final possibilities in the belief that he was moving forward when in fact he had merely been going around in a circle. The possibilities were repeating themselves in his mind. "Don't be silly," said a voice inside him, "you haven't a chance. The move you're chasing is an illusion, a piece of utter nonsense, a sheer stupidity quite unworthy of you."

The master straightened up and raised his eyes. His opponent wore an indulgent smile. The spectators were no longer interested in their game; they were now watching what was happening on the other boards. There was only one old man sitting opposite them in the front row; it was impossible to tell whether he was watching or dozing.

Then the master slowly stretched out his hand to make the inevitable move and advance the pawn one square to protect the king. Was it only this which was to have been the critical move in his career? His fingers trembled imperceptibly; otherwise, he was quite calm. He leaned back against the chair, frowned for a moment, and thought, "I probably wasn't wrong, there must have been such a move. Only I wasn't able to find it. I'm tired. It'll all come out in the commentaries." Suddenly he realized that he didn't care what the commentaries said, he didn't care what slips he had made and where they had been, and he didn't care that once again, and for the last time, he would not advance to the finals. Nothing mattered at all. A mood of calm overtook him. He moved the pawn.

He remembered the letter, opened it, and read it. His wife had written to him about perfectly ordinary matters, their health, the rainy weather. She made no mention of money. No doubt she had received the children's allowance (they had two children), and that would last her till the end of the month. That was good.

White moved.

"Check," said the master, moving his bishop to the other side.

It was a good thing his wife had not wished him luck in the game; it would have sounded ironic now. She hadn't the faintest idea what chess was all about. It bored her when he sat at home for hours over the board and spoke no word to her. And she did have the right to expect him to talk to her about the things that interested her, to ask him at least to take her out, to go for a walk, or to see a film.

White was not waiting long now.

"Check," said the master again.

Ah, his daughter had written on the other side. She was already quite grown-up, fourteen years old, her head full of clothes and cosmetics. She reminded him not to forget the blouse with the hand-embroidered sleeves, which he had promised to buy her. The master smiled. No, he wouldn't forget. He had saved some money from his daily allowance, and he would get a consolation prize; there would be enough money left to buy decent presents both for her and for his son. His thoughts suddenly shifted to something else. Perhaps if he had not set aside that money, if he had used it to buy himself more substantial meals, perhaps then he would have found the strength to make the effort needed to win this last point. But he rejected the thought at once, with a frown, as though it sickened him; he was to find how selfish a man can sometimes be and what terrible thoughts he can have, even about those who are closest to him.

White had found a position for his king.

"Check," said the master.

But this was the last time he could check. The white king had already found its way to safe shelter. The master reflected a while longer and then said quietly, "I resign." They filled in the papers together. On the demonstration board the notice "Black resigns" hung around the neck of his bishop.

The master did not start in on the postmortem of the game, as is usual with the loser, who wants to show how and where the game might have changed course and taken a turn in his favor. A loser does this more to calm his nerves and cover up his distress than to analyze the game. The master stood up straight away and cast a glance round the room. There was a moist brilliance in his eyes that could not quite be hidden by his outward calm. However, no one noticed this. Here the people watch the pieces, not the players.

JOVAN BOŠKOVSKI

The Man on the Roof

He first climbed up the attic steps onto the terrace that was used for drying clothes, and from there he clambered up onto the roof of the building. Suddenly he found himself in the midst of a sea of walls and roofs jutting out like frozen waves. From the top of the six-story block the view opened out over a great part of the town—jumbled clusters of rooftops with occasional slits where the streets cut their way through below, houses with ugly back walls, terraces and balconies sticking out at confused angles, and gray walls plunging down into a muddle of dirty back-yards.

He was alone on the roof—one man among the tarnished, faded pyramids of the rooftops and the cracked, moldy tiles, one man alone, standing above the houses and the streets and breathing in the first tentative hints of awakening that wafted up from the pavements still vibrating with the heat of the fierce afternoon July sun, now half-hidden behind the tall buildings on the skyline. He was alone here

---

Jovan Boškovski (1920–1968) was born of a poor family of migrant workers in Skopje. His formal education was interrupted after elementary school; thereafter he was able to continue his education only in night schools. He began to write long before the Second World War, but his work did not appear in print until 1944.

From that time, however, Jovan Boškovski published widely, both in literary journals and in newspapers. His stories—often realistic accounts of the events of recent Macedonian history—have been gathered in three collections, *Gunfire* (1947), *Blockade* (1950), and *People and Birds* (1955). His novel, *The Assassins of Salonika* (1961), is based upon a well-known story of the Ilinden uprising of 1903, during which Macedonians rose up against the Turkish oppressor, captured the mountain town of Kruševo and openly declared Macedonia a republic—a republic of revolutionary social aims which unfortunately could sustain itself for only ten days.

and closer to the sky and the silence of its barren, dry expanse. "How quiet it is here," he thought. So, at least, it
seemed to him at first. But if he had only paused to listen
to the sounds coming through that thin crust of concrete
that lay between him and the massive building below, he
would have been inundated by those same inaudible sounds
which were even now swirling and seething inside him:
the harsh crackle of the burnt-out radio set, the clattering
of dishes in the kitchen, his wife's fractious muttering, the
slamming of the door, all those unbearable sounds that had
concentrated into a maddening din inside his head and
driven him out onto this roof.

He was no more than two steps away from the edge of
the roof overhanging the abyss of the street. He took only
one step, but the momentum was enough to carry him on
easily into the second. He was immediately seized by the
giddy excitement and painful lightheadedness that heights
always brought on him, but he knew that this feeling sig-
naled no physical loss of balance, but only a crumbling of
some inner support when he faced the depth before him.
Far below him yawned the chasm of the street; he reached
back to the ridge of the roof and eased himself on his hands
and knees toward the iron scaffolding of a large neon advertisement—a few criss-cross iron bars haphazardly joined
together to support a circle of interwoven letters advertising
a brand of aspirin. The sign, which had been set up long
ago and since forgotten, stretched out uselessly across the
sky. One letter had fallen out of the vertical row, and the
bottom cross-bar was bent so that the whole circle was
slightly dented on one side, as if something had pressed
against it. It had long since given up shining at night,
and during the day it merely stood there, lost among the
rooftops.

The man caught hold of its iron scaffolding with both
hands as if he were crucified. Now he was able to look
down without feeling insecure. The people below were
miniature figures dotted over the pavement. Occasional cars

cut quickly across the white line down the middle of the road. Only a red bus, swinging boldly into the wide sweep of the square, moved on down the main street where it was forced to crawl slowly along its own fixed line.

Cautiously, as though testing the firmness of the iron rungs that supported him, he leaned out over the gulf of the street, and the iron bit even more sharply into the tender soles of his feet. He now stared straight down at the pavement in front of the building on which he was standing, straight down at the passers-by, whose figures now seemed still smaller. They might easily have been stuck into the ground, except that, as they moved farther into the distance, their upright position gradually became more evident.

It was most unlikely that any of them had noticed him, hidden as he was among the iron bars of the scaffolding, because none raised his eyes in this crushing afternoon heat —for the sun was still glaring fiercely. And so the man was able to gaze down to his heart's content, unseen in his vantage point above the chasm of the street.

He remembered that it was from just this place that a certain Professor Artur Schneider had strung a tightrope across to the building on the other side, the one with the ugly concrete eagle embellishing the top of the roof—the building that was no longer there. The tall, long-legged German with his wispy hair and sinewy legs used to do his tightrope act while carrying a long balancing pole like an oar. He walked between the two buildings while the people below craned their necks to watch him. Herr Professor Schneider used to walk above the street beside the very rooftops, well above the balconies, on a steel tightrope strung from one building to the other, and on this rope he performed his act and danced to the rhythm of Strauss waltzes. Far below him the people, packed closely together, gazed up, leaving a wide open furrow along the pavement under the entire length of the rope. They watched him evening after evening as he traversed the empty space between the two buildings, the dark sky eerily lit by spot-

lights. They watched him every evening and waited for
something to happen, something that was not part of his
complex and calculatedly dangerous capers on the wires.
They waited for that empty space to be filled with a cry—
their cry—and a solitary headlong fall—his fall. They
waited for the end of these regular evening acts on the tightrope. But it never happened. Then one day there was no
longer any wire, just as now there is no longer any building on the other side of the street.

Now the man was above this same empty space, the man
who at the time of Professor Schneider's visit had been a
child, gazing up wide-eyed, not daring to breathe, at the
seemingly inaccessible height marked by the edge of the
roof. Now he stood, bending forward but still clinging firmly to the iron rungs, leaning out confidently over the emptiness above the street. What if, now, he thought, what if,
now, I were to fill this empty space below me with my fall
and with a cry—their cry? What if those people speckled
along the sides of the street were to gather afterwards
around one dark shadow on the pavement? No music, no
glaring spotlights, only this soft, soundless fall, after which
nothing would be left but a dark stain on the pavement?

As though he were starting on that soft flight through
the emptiness, on that long drop into the depths, the man
curved his body out into an arch above the dizzying space.
The iron seared into his flesh and the sharp pain forced him
to make a sudden retreat, casting his body backward toward the security of the iron bars supporting his arms.

Below him, he knew, on the fourth floor, the burnt-out
radio would be crackling and spluttering. Other sounds had
begun to escape from the back yard and the open windows
of the apartments. His wife's voice could also be heard calling him; he recognized her voice fighting its way through
the general confusion of sounds. He stayed on the roof,
but he freed himself from the scaffolding of the aspirin
advertisement and drew back two paces from the edge.

His wife was calling him loudly from somewhere below, somewhere in the bowels of the building. But he did not answer her call, he did not go down to her; he stayed where he was on the roof. He glanced over the rooftops around him, through the jumble of crooked domes and upturned chimney pots; he stared at all this through the haziness of dusk. Then again he heard his wife calling him from the terrace.

"Milan, where are you? Why did you climb up there?"

"Come on up," he answered.

"You come down. What are you doing up there?"

"Come up. You'll see."

He went back to the terrace and stretched out both hands to help her up. As he hoisted her clumsily over the low wall, a slight tremor ran through her arms, as though some distant wave of fear had swept over her. Then she moved closer to the edge of the roof overlooking the street and shuddered with giddiness at the dizzying drop through the heavy haze of dusk down to the pavement, which she could not dare to see. She recoiled sharply toward her husband, so sharply that she bumped into him and clung to his body, panting feverishly and quite unable to control her trembling.

"Why are you standing here? Aren't you frightened?"

"No. What's there to be frightened of?"

His wife smothered a frightened cry.

"You . . . you seem to be thinking of something," she said.

"What on earth's got into your mind? Come, sit down here."

"This is the third time you've been up here. Whenever you're upset you climb up onto the roof."

"Listen, why don't you sit down?"

"No. Let's go downstairs. What's the point of being up here?"

"I don't know. . . . Let's sit here till it gets dark, then we'll go down," he answered, placing her beside him on

the rough concrete ledge between the roof and the terrace.
The concrete was beginning to lose the savage heat of the
sun.

Evening lay on the rooftops, enveloping them in a bluish-
white haze. Sharp irregularities sank into the gentleness of
the dusk. She ran her fingers over her husband's forehead
till she came to the deep parting in his hair. Her hand was
moist with his damp sweat, which had already begun to
cool. He stared with half-open eyes through the bars of
iron scaffolding that supported the advertisement, sense-
lessly crossed against the vault of the evening sky. He
sat beside his wife, silent and motionless. They would sit
like this in silence, until the stars began to glitter above
them. Then they would go downstairs, to the fourth floor.

PETRE M. ANDREEVSKI

The Vampire

Not even one night had passed since the burial of Nyden
Stoikoychin, and the dead man had already returned to the
village. How he had returned, why he had returned, whom
he wanted to spite, whether he had forgotten something, or
whether he had remembered something after his death,
nobody could tell. Some people claimed that his return had
been speeded by the negligence of his disconsolate wife,
Nydenica, who had forgotten to cleanse herself and throw
the water of the Notchesky's millstream over her shoulder.
Other people believed that he had attached himself to some
grief-stricken mourner as he turned back for a final parting
look at the graveyard.

There were all sorts of explanations for his return, although nobody was able to fathom what had brought him
back to the world. Was it simply his departed soul, or was
it something else? Although nobody had actually seen Nyden Stoikoychin, everybody felt his presence. Sometimes
he appeared as a sound of sniffing in the sultry heat of the
house and sometimes as a shadow, but most often he was

Petre M. Andreevski was born in the village of Sloeštica,
near Bitola, in 1934 and was educated in Bitola and Skopje. He
now lives in Skopje, where he is employed as a folk music editor
at Skopje Radio–TV. But he is best known as a poet—a writer of
narrative poems that are developed out of the legends and
mythologies of the Macedonian people. Since 1960 his poetry
has been collected in several volumes, and his recent poetic sequence, "The Death of the Guiser," was honored at the Struga
International Poetry Festival of 1971 as the best Macedonian
poem of the year.

Andreevski has also published a collection of short stories,
On the Seventh Day (1964). In them, as in the story presented
here, he has made use of materials similar to those with which
his poetry has become associated.

113

something that brushed the back of your neck, whistled up your trouser legs, and blew down your sleeves. He began to appear in all the places he had visited before his sudden death. He would often ruin the gardens by driving in the cattle and letting them trample over the vegetable patches. Sometimes he would take to the hills on horseback, for whenever a horse came back sweating all over and frothing at the mouth everybody knew that Nyden had been riding it. God only knows what else those people went through that summer, the longest of all summers. No sooner would they sit down to dinner than a spoon nobody was holding would be raised in front of their eyes, dipped into the food, and carried through the air. The people would sit stock-still, gaping with horror, their mouths full of unmasticated food. Occasionally some of the older folk would pluck up enough courage to call in Nydenica and beg her to pray Nyden to stop his campaign of terror. She did as they asked and implored him to stop, but the people were still not satisfied. "Pray harder," they told her. "Pray harder."

"Leave us, Nyden, go back to your grave," she begged him again and again. "O Lord, why would You not take him as he was, why will You not accept his soul?" Nydenica prayed in her distress while the people glowered, grim and despondent, the dark pupils of their eyes overflowing with the blackness of the night. They trembled like reeds in the wind, and yet their bodies were motionless. Only their eyes moved. A cold shiver ran through them from head to toe whenever a window creaked, as Nyden, yielding to his wife's prayers, slipped outside. Their shiver spread until it filled the whole room. At the very moment that Nyden left them, all the dogs in the village started barking. It was an ear-splitting din, enough to raise the heavens and to be heard even beyond the hills, which were almost a day's ride from the village. "This damned barking, it will undermine our houses," the people muttered to themselves, blocking their ears and stopping their breath. And the river also stopped; some people saw it happen. It did not run dry, it simply stopped flowing and stood still in its bed. "What tracks do you leave for the dogs?" whispered Nydenica. "What makes them bark at you? Why is it they see you when you cannot be seen anywhere, Nyden?"

Nobody had a wink of sleep right through that hellish summer. Sleep could not supplant the fear of being strangled, of being whirled away in the vortex of a hurricane, of being carried downstream by a turbulent river, of being left to awaken in a tall, lonely tree. Anyone who did manage to doze off could scarcely have closed his eyes before he would leap up with a yell, as though iron-shod hooves were trampling over him, as though a great bodiless weight were crushing him. Everybody would gather round and offer him sweetened water to drink. Then they would all cleanse themselves in the smoke of some dry, foul-smelling grasses, which brought tears to their eyes and made them cough painfully, as though they were releasing the pain of long nights of wakefulness.

Nydenica herself lived through fearful nights. How she suffered! She longed each night for day to break, because her nights were the longest in the world. It was Nyden who made them unbearable by climbing up the stairs, scratching at the windows, opening doors and cellars, stirring up the embers in the fireplace. And oh, how long those nights were when he would crawl into her bed and a heavy weight would press down upon her! At such moments she would first try to persuade herself that it was nothing more than the weight of the blanket and would immediately try to throw it off. But the effort was agonizing, and even after she had freed herself from the blanket the heavy weight continued to crush her. After this struggle she would plead once more with her husband: "Go away, Nyden. Don't torment me, Nyden. Be as good as you once were when your own legs brought you home. What brings you now, Nyden, the darkness or the wind?"

Even while she was praying, Nydenica could hear a voice saying, "Where can I go, my dear wife, where can I return to, when I have not come from anywhere?" It was, in fact, Nydenica who uttered these words, partly as a reproach and partly as a meaningless consolation. Only when the weight was lifted from her did she know that Nyden had given in to her pleading and moved to some other part of the room.

Some nights he would enter her home several times and bring her sweets stolen from Vidan Siveski's café. "Good God, how on earth can he carry them?" Nydenica wondered. "What hands does he hold them in when his hands are buried beneath the ground? What pockets does he hide them in, and how can he get them out when the café is locked?" But one way or another he brought her the sweets. They would suddenly hail down from above, through the cloying air, fall into the middle of the room, and scatter in all directions. Sometimes they would drop into her lap, and then beads of sweat would break out on her chin, under her arms, all over. "I can't eat stolen sweets, Nyden, not even if it makes you angry. I'm going to give them back to the café owner," said Nydenica, her tongue furred with fear. And she returned them many times.

"I never thought he'd steal from me," mumbled Vidan Siveski, his pencil tucked behind his ear. "I never thought a man like that, who'd spent his whole life fighting against thieves, would turn to stealing."

"Forgive him, Vidan," said Nydenica. "Who knows what it's like for him? He walks among men, but nobody sees him. Maybe night and day are one and the same for him, and nobody would know what to do with so much time, nobody would even know how to make a start."

"Maybe you're right," answered Vidan Siveski, the café owner. "Maybe even the dead need friends. But why did he have to turn to stealing to fill up his time?"

"Forgive him, Vidan," Nydenica repeated, "I'll return everything to you; I'll give back everything he steals from you."

Ah, but Nyden Stoikoychin did not steal only from Vidan

Siveski's café. He robbed all the houses in the village. A sheaf of corn was missing from the Netchkovskis' and was found on Nydenica's threshing floor. Some people swore that they had clearly seen the sheaf of corn flying over the village and coming to land by Nydenica's house. The Plevneshovskis lost a donkey and found it hitched to a post in Nydenica's stables. The Bubushovskis were short a bale of tobacco and a quantity of apples they had saved for wedding celebrations; the Kvachkovskis lost a cartload of pumpkins, the Jonovskis three strings of onions and a string of hot peppers, the Shvrgovskis all their colored yarn for knitting stockings as well as several baskets of cornel berries, eggs, and hazelnuts. As before, everything was found at Nydenica's. She returned everything, right down to the tiniest trifle, and sometimes, even when live people had stolen from one another, she would return things which had not been found at her house. She continued to return as many things as she could, but soon she was no longer able.

So the people began to protest. "We don't want a woman in this village who keeps company with the Fiends," they shouted, flocking before her house. "Where do you hide the things he steals?"

"Is it only hatred that brings you to me?" asked Nydenica. Then she folded her arms across her breast and swore by heaven and by the stars that she had nothing and she knew nothing.

"Don't swear false oaths," shouted someone in the crowd. "God is our witness that we have not slept the whole year, that our cattle have wasted away, and our food supplies are exhausted."

"We've had enough of fear; we've had enough of theft!" the people shouted.

"Since you will not believe me, my people, tell me at least what I can do to make amends. Tell me what I can do," repeated Nydenica, wiping her moist face.

"Get out of here. Take yourself to the place where sickness dwells and the phantoms gather," they shouted, "or else find the money for us to pay a man who is able to see vampires, because only a man who is able to see vampires knows how to kill them."

Nydenica swore again that she had no way of getting the money, and that Nyden, if he had known that he would have to be killed even after his death, would certainly have left some money behind. But the people remembered Nydenica's fields and told her she would have to sell them. "Then how will I be able to live?" asked Nydenica.

"Don't try to save him with your tears," the people cried. "You can die of hunger just as we have been dying of fear all year."

Three days later they brought to the village a man who could see vampires. God knows how they found him, or where they brought him from, but he was led into the village and given a gun immediately. When dark fell and the dogs began their fearful barking, everybody knew that Nyden Stoikoychin was coming into the village. So the man with the gun went out to hunt for him. The people followed him and were filled with unease like the night, like the barking of the dogs, like the river which had stopped flowing, which had not run dry but had simply stopped flowing and stood still in its bed.

"There he is!" whispered the man who could see vampires. "He's already seen me. He's trying to run away. He's climbed onto the roof of the cowshed—now he's jumped onto the granary. He's trying to hide in the barn. He's trying to turn himself into a spider, a cockroach, or a moth, but he cannot. Now he's scuttling over the threshing floor!" Then the man suddenly stopped dead, raised his gun, and fired. The shot echoed through the dark, careened over the fields, ricocheted off the hills, and sped back from the mountains. This shot seemed to release some tension in the night and to bring relief from a heavy, invisible weight. The dogs stopped barking, and the river began to flow once again.

"How did he hide his blood?" the people wondered as they walked back home. "How did he carry it?" They were whispering about the blood that had been spilled and spattered over Nydenica's threshing floor.

The following day Nydenica's barn was teeming with people. Men and women, old and young, halt and lame, all were pushing, shoving, jostling, some were craning their necks or jumping up and down to get a better look, others were shouting, pushing through the throng, to see the blood of Nyden Stoikoychin and to witness his second death. But there on the threshing floor, stretched out in a pool of blood, surrounded by the crowd, lay Nydenica. She lay there with a bullet through her heart, her eyes wide open and gazing up at the sky, and a smile upon her face. Death could not have made anyone seem lovelier or happier.

"She obviously had to be shot before he could be killed," said one old man.

"But what is left hidden in her heart?" the people asked, as they looked up at the hills from which, like a summer torrent, like a noisy flood, the people from the neighboring villages came streaming.

The Women on the Little Wooden Stools

The men who live in this building come out onto their balconies early in the evening, and, around sunset, they rest their chins on the hot plaster of the balcony wall and let the red rims of the hills sink into the pupils of their eyes. Above their heads babies' diapers, inflamed by the redness of the sky, yearn for water. The men who live in this building and who rest their chins on the warm balcony walls in the evening, with the babies' diapers, dark and thirsty, always hanging above their heads are not always apathetic. Sometimes they half lower their eyelids, squeezing down the red rims of the hills; then their wives come out, bringing with them the smell of the kitchen or else sniveling children to get tangled among legs. Then, as the cries rise from the children rolling on the trampled grass in the yards, the twilight fades in the pupils of their eyes.

*   *   *   *

Taško Georgievski was born in 1935 in the village of Kron-čelovo in "Aegean Macedonia" (as the Yugoslav Macedonians call that part of northern Greece which, at least until 1945, had a dominantly Slavic population). Like many of the Slavs living in Greece, he came into Yugoslavia in 1943. He lived first near Prilep in the village of Dolneni, then he was settled, along with other refugees, in the Vojvodina (in Eastern Serbia near the Hungarian border). He returned to Macedonia in 1952 and has since been living in Skopje, where he received his education both in secondary school and at the Faculty of Philosophy. He was first employed as a journalist there; now (like so many of his fellow writers) he occupies a position at Skopje Radio–TV.

Georgievski published his first collection of short stories in 1957 and a second nearly ten years later. Since 1957, however, he has written four novels, the most distinguished, *Black Seed* (1962), concerning the Civil War in Greece at the end of the Second World War. He has also written several radio dramas.

For a long time a dull blow echoed in the space between the two doors, resounding with a strange resonance until it could be perceived in the adjacent room. Then this strange hammering on the outer door dissolved in the buzzing of the flies that had slipped in through the broken window and gathered in swarms. Some of them settled on the writer's hand, tickling his skin with the sticky pads of their feet and making him attenuate the letters he was writing. He did not bother to get up and unbolt the door but simply asked, staring out somewhere high among the leaves of the poplar in front of his window, "Who is it?"

"Are you in there?"

Now he had no choice but to stand up and draw the bolt with which the door had been locked from inside. It was the wife of a technical engineer at the printing press; the words had coiled in through the empty keyhole straight to where he was sitting and had tickled him behind the ears. When the door smiled hoarsely open on its rusty hinges, his eyes were smothered by the image of two bulging breasts; the pen in the penholder squeaked painfully as it scraped across the coarse surface of the door. "D'you need your frying pan?"

In the neat pleats of her light-colored dress—whatever color it was there in the patterned half-shadow—there was far more modesty than in her voice. And the pen was still scratching painfully against the slats of the door. The buzzing flies even brought into the room the almost inaudible rustling of the green leaves of the poplar standing outside the broken window.

"No, you can take it."

He went to the pantry to fetch the frying pan, and when

In this story Georgievski makes use of an image that has been familiar and suggestive to the Aegean imagination for almost three thousand years—the image of old women sitting in a doorway. These women, who still provide a running commentary on the life around them, here provide a choric commentary for Georgievski, as they have for many writers before him.

he came out he was followed by the choking smell of rancid fat. He knew that after all this, after this smell, after
these bulging breasts which bewitched him with their whiteness, he would not be able to write about the people from
this building, no matter how poetic their life might be.
Later, after she had gone out the door, smiling hoarsely on
its hinges, even after the clip-clop of her clogs had faded
away, he was not able to shake off the smell of rancid fat,
which had almost choked him when he was taking the pan
off the hook in the pantry. While he was refreshing himself
under the tap he decided it would be better to write sep-
arately about each person in the building rather than describe them all together, for he would not be able to capture
all the chattering drops of water that trickled off his head
into the basin. And the whiteness of her breasts seemed to
seep out of every pore, turning into porcelain milk in the
basin. The basin had a strange sheen. The white towel
drank in the drops of water. Phew! It's so damn hot and
sultry you simply can't relax, and she just goes clip-clopping
around in her clogs. Just as he was about to sit down at the
table the sound of wood rapping on wood returned, faintly
at first. Then, as he was ready to start writing again, the
quivering thread of her voice slipped in through the empty
keyhole: "Ha, ha, ha, heee, I'm taking my husband his
lunch now. He can't come home; it's too far." And, after
her footsteps had faded away, round the back of the other
building, his ears picked up the sound of the voices of the
women who sit at the entrance on little wooden stools, their
skirts hitched up over their knees. "She's going to take her
husband his potato; then she'll come back to borrow a frying pan from the man upstairs. Ha, ha, ha!"

It was the hour when the building cast no shadow in any
direction. He left the page he was writing and went into the
pantry; he was enveloped by the smell of onions, paprikas,
and pickled red tomatoes. Hunger, he thought, had stimu-
lated the very juices which run through the muscle and
marrow, and this awareness gave him immense satisfaction.

He turned on the stove, and soon pieces of paprika were spluttering in the hot fat. An inexplicable fit of anger seized him, and he began beating time with the spoon on the edge of the frying pan: tic-a-tac-tac-tac-tac. He did not hear the outside door being opened, even though the rusty lock chuckled hoarsely as it was eased to one side. He did not turn round until he heard her voice right behind him, and as he did so he was first aware of the valley between the bulging breasts.

"You making lunch?"

"As you can see."

It suddenly became unbearably stuffy in the pantry. Beads of sweat broke out on his forehead and poured down his face. And behind them, somewhere in the room, the flies were buzzing about, startled by the noise. He felt her glance piercing him like countless needles, pricking his heart, and forcing it to beat faster. He was waiting for her to say "I need a pan"; he was waiting for her to say, to say, to say, "Lend me a knife." But she kept on smiling, and her smile, mingled with that look, enveloped him like something warm and damp. All the fat seemed to have vaporized in the frying pan; it had become close and stuffy in the pantry. Those currents of animal juices from his bones and muscles must have dried up and turned into something which stuck in his throat. But she did not say, "Give me some salt"; she did not say, say, say, "Let me have a knife, at least, to cut the bread." She had simply bolted the outer door when she had come in.

The sultriness had hung in the building for several days, stifling, damp, and hot. It was, quite simply, a stuffy heat in a cramped pantry where it was impossible to avoid touching. The paprikas had burnt and would soon turn into black cinders. He had opened all the windows in the little room, but the smell of burnt fat would not go away, and that smell which hung about the entrance would never be driven away, because it had soaked into the women who sat on the little wooden stools, their skirts hitched up over

their knees. And the men in their silence, seemingly en-
chanted by the twilight, would look down inquisitively
when they heard the voices of the women who still would
be sitting on the little wooden stools, their skirts hitched
up over their knees, and from time to time they would toss
a remark from one balcony to another. "The printer's
missus made him burn his paprikas. Ha, ha, ha!"

A few days later, when the sun was past its zenith and
his room had come into the shade, he was sitting at the
table playing dominoes with the technical engineer from
the printing-house. He was staring at the little black pieces
with their white dots and losing every time. The printer
laughed out loud: Ah, my friend, don't you laugh, he
thought, I don't dare look you in the eyes. If I did, I'd be
able to read your thoughts, and then I wouldn't lose. He
really did not dare to raise his eyes; even to himself he was
mean and shabby. But was he, after all, to blame when it
had been so stuffy, so nauseating that day? When he had
been forced to duck his head under the tap to cool off his
overheated blood? And she—he had expected she would
ask him to do her some small service, no matter what—
lend her a toothpick even—but she had simply come in and
bolted the door from the inside and then wanted to see if
the bed had strong springs and to determine whether it
touched the floor under the weight of two people.

"Six and four."

"Six and six."

With this move he managed to stop the printer from fin-
ishing out and winning. They stopped playing. He excused
himself by saying that he was thinking of going out and
that it was time to get changed. Later, when he was alone,
quite alone, he laughed aloud when he heard the women on
their little wooden stools at the entrance asking, "What!
Did you give him back his frying pan?" and when he heard
the printer's mumbled answer: "No, we were just playing
dominoes." But when he leaned again over the table and
read the pages he had written, he tore them up and flung

them out of the window. The little pieces seeded themselves around the roots of the poplar. This all helped to relieve him. It now seemed senseless to him to write about the men who sit on their balconies in the warm evenings, resting their chins on the warm plaster while the red rims of the hills swim in their eyes, and to forget about everything else that goes on behind closed doors, bolted from inside. Finally, he began to feel quite superfluous in that room, and, when the wooden stairs announced with a creak that he was going down, he decided that nobody need ever write about any of this. If anybody wants to know something about the suburbs he must cross the railway embankment himself and look at the women who sit on little wooden stools, their skirts hitched up over their knees, because they have soaked up the smells that force their way through the empty keyholes and get in behind locked doors. In the town the twilight is rose-colored and does not carry anything with it through the town toward the red rims of the hills, because just above the railway embankment there constantly floats a curtain of sparks left by the locomotives. One has to cross the embankment to see how the day fans out across the sky and fades to the cries of children sucking stems of grass.

He walked toward the town, followed by countless eyes that twinkled on the balconies and in front of every entrance.

The Witness

"Why d'you make me wear these shoes, Mama?" said the child. "They're too tight for me, and I can't walk in them." He screwed up his face in pain.

"We're going to the police station," said his mother. "They want to talk to you."

"Can't you tell them, Mama?" said the child.

"It's you they want to ask. Be sensible and mind what you say," his mother warned him.

They walked through the village; people looked at the child and said nothing. Some even began to follow. The child looked around, frightened. The peasants watched him with inquisitive eyes as they drew closer and closer.

"My shoes are pinching me," said the child. "I'll take them off so we can hurry."

"There's no need to hurry, my son," said his mother. "And remember, you must tell them everything they want to know."

When they reached the town hall, a policeman showed them to a room on the second floor. "The boy's to go in by himself," he said as he opened the door.

The magistrate looked up at the boy.

"Let the mother in as well," he said. "Now, young fellow, what's your name?" the magistrate asked.

Meto (Metodija) Fotev was born in 1932, in the village of Ljubojno near Lake Prespa, in southwest Macedonia. He was educated in local schools and at the teachers' college in Bitola, and taught for a time thereafter. Then, in 1954, he came to Skopje to work as a journalist with *Nova Makedonija*, the daily newspaper, and later at Skopje Radio–TV, where he is presently a drama editor. He began publishing his stories in 1955 and has since won prizes for two of his novels, *Kat's Descendants* (1966) and *Villages and Soldiers* (1969).

"Gere," the child replied.

"How old are you, Gere?"

"I'm six. That's why I still don't go to school," said Gere. The child could see about ten people in the room.

"Sit down here, Gere," said the magistrate.

Somebody told the policeman to go outside and stand by the door, for voices could be heard coming from the corridor.

"You were with Villant, weren't you Gere?" asked the magistrate.

"Yes, I was with Villant," answered the child.

"Tell me what you were doing." The magistrate was a good man and had a pleasant sounding voice. "Tell me everything Gere, just as it happened."

"When Mummy was naked in the bath . . . ," began Gere.

"Shame on you, Gere," said his mother.

The child thought his mother was afraid he might forget to tell something, that he might leave out some detail. Then he remembered he ought to mention his father as well, because his mother might get angry with him for speaking only about her.

"Daddy was also naked in the bath," continued Gere. "And when Mummy had finished bathing Ilka, she told Daddy to put on a white shirt. Ilka was crying because the soap got into her eyes. I didn't cry; I never, never cry."

"And then what happened?" asked the magistrate impatiently.

"Then Mummy bathed me too," the child went on. "She didn't dress me in new clothes, but she dressed Ilka in a new blouse. My mother put on a new dress, then my father picked up Ilka, and my mother took me by the hand. My mother told me that they were going to a wedding and that I would be staying with Villant because Villant's mother was also going to the wedding."

"Did you want to stay with Villant, Gere?" asked the magistrate.

"Yes, I did. Villant and I talk together and play games.

He's got hundreds of toys and lets me play with all of them."

"How old was Villant?" asked the magistrate of a man seated behind the desk.

"Twenty-three," said Villant's mother through her tears.

"What sort of toys were they, Gere?" asked the magistrate.

"All sorts," said the child. "American toys."

Villant's mother burst into tears again. Gere did not know what else to say. He looked at his mother. She was standing quietly, her thumbs hooked into the top of her apron.

"Granny says that Villant broke his back when he fell from a horse," the child went on. "And first he had to lie in bed, then his father sent him a wheel chair from America. He's also got a little tool-box with fret saws and hammers. Boro knows the names of all the other toys."

"And don't you know what they're called?" asked the magistrate.

"Let Boro tell something as well," said Gere.

A man went out of the room. Gere felt utterly alone. He would have liked to run over and cling to his mother, but he noticed that he had worked his feet out of his shoes while talking to the magistrate, and he felt ashamed to run across the room in his socks.

"There's no need to stand like that," said the magistrate to the people in the room. "Sit down. If there aren't enough chairs for everybody, we'll have some brought in."

The people settled themselves on the chairs and benches. Gere's heart was fluttering with fright. It might easily happen, he remembered, that Boro could not be found at home. He's a great one for roving around, thought Gere, he's never in the same street twice. Gere's mother looked at her son. Gere looked back at her and she smiled at him. Then his mother suddenly lowered her head. The magistrate was questioning the peasants about the harvest. They told him it had gone well.

"The Germans have gone, and the other Fascists too," said the magistrate. "And the droughts have gone with them."

Boro entered first, followed by his father. Boro was a sprightly slip of a boy. He was fiddling with his slingshot, not knowing where to put it. He had no doubt forgotten to hide it on the way. He turned to his father and handed him the slingshot. His father gave an embarrassed laugh and stuffed it into his pocket.

"Are you Boro?" asked the magistrate.

"I am Boro Iliyevsky," answered the child.

"What's that thing which spins round and smokes when you press a button?" said Gere to Boro.

"Ventilitator," said Boro.

"I know that," said Gere. "And that other one which sings when you pick up the earpiece?" said Gere.

"Detectator," said Boro.

"I knew that too," said Gere. "Boro and I—we both know."

"You don't know how to say detectator," said Boro. Gere blushed. But he was glad all the same that Boro had come.

"Boro's smaller than me," said Gere. "And once he broke Villant's fret saw."

"It broke itself," said Boro. "Now Villant's deaded," he added. Gere burst into tears. All of a sudden he burst into tears.

"Now, now, Gere, you're a big strong man aren't you?" said the magistrate.

"That always makes him start crying," said Gere's mother. "You just need to mention it. He does nothing but cry these days."

"Aren't you going to tell us about Villant, Gere?" asked the magistrate.

"Yes, I am," said the child.

"What were you doing that day, you and Villant?"

"He was teaching me how to write," said Gere.

"Do you know how to write?" asked the magistrate.

"Yes, I do. I know how to write 'Villant,' " said Gere. "I don't know anything else."

"He knows how to write on wood with a penknife," said Boro.

"And Villant was reading. I took the earphones and listened to music. I was lying on the bed with the deductator," said Gere. Boro sniggered.

"Villant said to me, 'Shall I read aloud?' And I said to him, 'All right.' Then Villant read and I listened. 'It's hot' he said. I went out to switch on the ventilator. But Villant said the batteries were dead. Then Villant threw the book on the bed and said, 'Let's play.' He went with Utopina to the door where there was no window."

"Who's this Utopina?" the magistrate asked.

"Villant's wheel chair," Boro interrupted.

"We broke a bottle on his wheel chair when we christened it," said Gere. "I'll be the godfather," said Villant. "All right," I said. "Then Villant told me great travel adventures and many other things. And he told me to break the bottle on the handrest. I broke the bottle and it shattered into bits. Then Villant's mother appeared and asked us what we were doing. Villant told her his bottle of vitamins had broken. 'Watch out you don't get hurt,' she said, 'and pick up the bits of glass.' So I picked up the bits and Villant's mother whispered to me to go. 'Villant's going to sleep,' she told me. But Villant said to her, 'Mother, leave me alone with Gere.' "

"Why did you break the bottle?" Boro asked, puzzled.

"That's how boats are christened," said Gere.

"And what did you do next?" asked the magistrate.

"Villant said, 'We'll make a flag for Utopina,' " Gere continued.

"No, not then; that day when Villant went to the door with his wheel chair," said the magistrate.

"We were playing our game. Villant showed me this game

and nobody else knows about it. He went over to the door and I sat beside him and we didn't say a word. You could hear footsteps in the street. 'This is . . . this is . . . Pavle,' said Villant. I ran over to the window and sure enough there was Pavle. He was walking down the street carrying a spade over his shoulder. 'It's Pavle,' I said to Villant. Villant smiled. I sat down again and we kept quiet again. 'Somebody's coming,' said Villant. I didn't hear anything. 'Who's this?' said Villant. I wanted to go to the window, but Villant told me to stop, and then he stared up at the ceiling. 'It's Stojna,' he said. I went to the window. It really was Stojna. 'She goes to Demo the goatherd at night,' said Villant. 'Everyone goes somewhere at night,' he said. 'Everyone in the village.' "

"Gere," said his mother. "What did I tell you on the way here?"

"Just you go on with your story," said the magistrate reassuringly. One could see that the magistrate was beginning to grow interested in the story Gere was telling. "Now tell us everything, young fellow."

"Everyone goes somewhere at night, that's what Villant told me," said Gere. "The girls also go out. They first go to bed, then at midnight they go out. They make their arrangements during the day while they're working, and at night they go off with someone. Every night it's somebody different. I asked Villant where they go. He told me they go riding."

"Comrade Magistrate!" said one of the members of the village council.

"It's all part of Villant's psychology," said the magistrate. "Everything must be heard, comrades. Everything must be recorded. Now, what sort of a name is this—Villant?" asked the magistrate.

"The last time his father came back from America," said one of the members of the council, "he stayed two years in the village. A child was born to him and he christened it

Villant. Then he left for America and he's still out there."

Nobody in the room spoke. One could feel that every-body wanted Gere to speak.

"He's rolling in cash," the man continued.

"Ah, comrades, all you can think of is money," said the magistrate. "Tell me now, Gere, what happened after this?"

Gere knew that Villant was now dead. Yet he simply could not imagine that he would never see him again. He could not believe in his friend's death. Then Gere recalled what had happened. He could have talked for days.

" 'Let's play the letter game,' Villant said to me. I sat down on the bed and said to him, 'I'll ask first.' 'You ask first,' said Villant—'but only from things that can be found in the room.' I gave him the letter 'U.' Villant thought about it and then said he didn't know. 'It's our Utopina,' I said. 'One to nothing,' I said. Then Villant said the letter 'H.' I thought it over and said 'air.' 'You're wrong this time, Gere,' said Villant. 'The letter "H," like in "head." ' 'Head,' I said. 'It's not head,' said Villant. Then he said, 'I'll tell you, but you mustn't breathe a word to anyone. Not a soul. Come over here,' he said. 'Move the rug.' I moved the rug and saw there was a hole in the floorboards. 'That doesn't count,' I said, 'it can't be seen.' Villant told me to lie down and look through the hole with one eye. And when I lay down and looked I could see his mother's bed. 'You mustn't tell a soul,' said Villant. 'I promise I won't,' I said. 'I know,' he said. 'When the postman brings father's letters, I peep through this hole,' said Villant, 'and watch him lying in bed with my mother. She always asks him loudly if he wants a glass of brandy, and they lie down on the bed. Then they sit up again, and my mother offers him another glass of brandy, loud enough for me to hear. Sometimes the post-man comes twice a day. He even comes in the evening.' Then I asked Villant how he could see, how he could get out of the wheel chair. And Villant went to the bed and took a hollow reed. He came back to the hole and fitted the reed into it. You could see everything. Then Villant said to me, 'Now I've told you everything. I've even told you about this, so there's nothing left I haven't told you. If you knew how to read,' he said to me, 'we could read together.' I promised him I wouldn't tell a soul. 'I know,' he said. Then he told me to go down and take the letter from the table. 'The postman came yesterday,' he said, 'and brought a letter. My mother didn't have time to read it. Because she spent so long in bed with the postman. Then some woman called her, and she got up and went out into the yard. She went away with that woman, and then the postman also went away, and the letter was left unread.' "

"This child's a brute!" shouted Villant's mother. "He's nothing but a bag of lies—this damned child. Why won't you let my poor Villant rest in peace?"

"Villant told me." Gere was also in tears now. "He gave the postman two pairs of trousers. And you gave him sugar. Villant told me; and coffee and flour."

"I'll have to ask you to leave, comrade," said the magistrate to Villant's mother, "if you can't keep quiet."

Everyone now began to grow afraid of the boy Gere. Nobody dared look him in the eyes for fear he might say something about them too. Everybody knew that Villant had known all the village secrets. However, they all believed the crippled boy had not opened his mouth to anyone. Gere's mother was white as a sheet. "I'm not a trained judge," said the magistrate. "I never finished any kind of schooling. But I still know that the truth must be told. That's the way it is, comrades." And he mopped his face with a handkerchief made of parachute silk.

Gere was still crying. He did not know what to do, so he continued: "Then I went down for the letter and shouted up to Villant, 'The door's locked, Villant.' He shouted down to tell me that the key was under the red flowerpot. I found the key there and opened the door and took the letter up to him. Villant opened it and read it. Then he came over to me and took my hand and said, 'My father's coming.' "

"When's he coming?" asked Villant's mother. "Tell me
—when?"

"I don't know," said Gere. "Villant dropped the letter
in between some books. Then he said to me, 'Sit down on
the bed, Gere; sit down and we'll sing.' He wheeled himself over to the bed in Utopina and put his hand on my
shoulder and we sang. I didn't shout very loud at first. Then
Villant said we should sing louder and we both gave it the
gas."

"That's quite true," said one of the peasants. "They were
kicking up a hell of a din. I happened to be passing their
window at the time. They were yelling their heads off."

"Then Villant said to me, 'I've learned how to torture myself. Let's go up to the Farmakov's yard and look around.' "
Gere simply could not stop talking. He was afraid that somebody might stop him, that some detail of his friend's life
might not be brought to light.

"We looked into the yard. Every day Vida used to come
and show herself at the barn window. Cvetko would always
come after Vida and wander up and down the granary, gazing at her. And Vida would watch him too, and smile. Then
she would take a quick look round the yard, turn back to
him, unbutton her blouse, and shove one breast through the
bars of the window. Cvetko's eyes would turn all watery as
he looked at Vida's breast. She would laugh at him and kiss
the iron grill over the window. Then she would unbutton
her blouse even farther, turn the other way, and push her
other breast through the bars. I don't know why it didn't
hurt when she squeezed her breast through the bars, but
she just laughed. Then Cvetko would cover his face with
his hands and stand there like that without moving. And
when he took his hands away, you could see he had been
crying. Vida also used to cry! But it wasn't like proper crying. Once Villant said to me, 'Those two know what great
love means. That's the greatest love, my friend.' "

"That's not true," said one of the peasants. "It's a bare-faced lie, Comrade Magistrate. God knows where this little monkey picks up all his stories. Everybody in the village knows that those two families can't stand the sight of each other. They're always at each other's throats, I'm telling you. And when the children are born—it's the same in both families—they suck poisoned milk and grow up hating each other. The Farmakovs and the Pelinkovs—who doesn't know about them? If you tried to tell me the lake had filled with gold overnight, I'd believe you—but I can't believe this story. Why, look at the names we've given them, Farmakov and Pelinkov. They were given these names because they hate each other so much. The boy's lying, Comrade Magistrate."

Young Gere remembered the day when Villant had first suggested spying on the Farmakovs' yard. He raised his head and saw the peasants looking scornfully at him.

"And even the very first time we saw them," said Gere, "Vida was at the window, and Cvetko was in the granary. Cvetko was in a filthy mood. He looked angrily at Vida, then he unbuttoned his fly as if he was going to piss over the fence. 'He's going to piss in the yard,' I said to Villant. 'No he isn't, Gere,' said Villant. 'That's just his way of showing how he hates her.' Vida was standing at the window holding onto the iron bars. They both stood just as they were, watching each other. Suddenly Vida unbuttoned her blouse and shoved her breast through the bars. Her breast, when we saw it then for the first time, was whiter than white, even up in the shadow under the gutter it was shiny white. Cvetko didn't know what to do. Vida was laughing, just like Sophia when I saw her once lying in the hay. Cvetko hung his head and buttoned up his fly. When he looked up again, his eyes were full of water. Not like when you're crying. It was pure water—you could see. I wanted to ask Villant why he had done this, but Villant told me to keep quiet. Cvetko looked at Vida and laughed. They stayed as they were for a long time. Cvetko didn't shift from his place in the granary, but Vida pressed against the bars with all her strength until her breast was hanging right out and the bars were cutting deep into her flesh. Somebody called Cvetko from down below. He waved and went down. Vida straightened up, pulled in her breast, and stuffed it back into her dress. 'Gere, my friend,' said Villant, 'we have been witnesses to the birth of a great love. But I still find it hard,' he said, 'to move away from the window.' 'Why,' I asked. 'You don't know, Gere. My eyes will never fill with water like Cvetko's.' "

The peasants and the magistrate stayed silent. All looked at the boy. Nobody looked at him scornfully.

" 'Cvetko's eyes were not full of water,' I said to Villant. 'Yes, they were,' he replied. From then on I knew that Cvetko's eyes were full of water. Every day when we watched them in the Farmakov's yard, it seemed to me that Cvetko's eyes were watery. If Villant said so, then it must be. He doesn't lie. He knows everything."

"Villant's deaded now," Boro suddenly remembered.

And his voice brought something new into the room. Gere looked ahead, his eyes were full of tears, but he wasn't crying.

"Gere, my son," said the magistrate, "tell us what else happened that day."

" 'I can only love with my soul, Gere . . .,' Villant said."

"Not then," said the magistrate. "Tell me about the day when the marriage took place."

" 'Come on,' said Villant, 'let's go and have a laugh.' 'I can't laugh,' I told him. 'Come, Gere; you're my best friend. Come, let's have a laugh. Don't you want to learn how to laugh?' And when Villant cried, I cried too. He stroked my hair. 'There, there,' he said, 'never mind.' "

Gere broke off and fell silent. Villant's mother was crying. Gere's mother was also crying, and then, for no apparent reason, she stood up from the bench where she had been sitting beside Boro.

"Go on with your story, Gere," said the magistrate.

"After that we didn't speak at all. The young people

were passing down the street singing, and Villant didn't say anything. I was walking behind Villant holding on to Utopina. I wasn't able to speak. 'Don't you feel hungry, Gere?' Villant asked me. I told him I didn't want anything to eat. Villant told me he had a box of sweets. I told him I didn't even want sweets.''

Gere began to cry. Then he began to sob and shake, as though he had been swimming in the lake in winter. The magistrate stood up and came over to the boy.

"Gere, my son, what's the matter?" he asked. "You musn't cry while you're telling us all about your friend. You must never cry, because Villant will get angry if you do."

"I'm not crying," said Gere.

"Then what happened, Gere? Come on, Gere; you're a big lad. You know everything. Try to remember what happened afterwards." The magistrate spoke gently.

" 'One day we'll go for a walk through the village, Gere,' said Villant, 'you and I together.' I told him I'd like to walk through the village. 'You'll be beside me, Gere,' said Villant, 'and we'll set off down the street. We'll see our friends, and then we'll go to the meadow.' Then Villant turned to me, 'D'you agree?' he said. 'I want to be with you the whole day in the meadow,' I told him. 'Gere,' said Villant, 'what'll we take with us for our journey?' 'I don't know,' I told him. 'Never mind, I'll take care of that,' said Villant. 'But what a journey this'll be, Gere. Tell me, would you like to go all the way to the spring by the willows?' 'Oh yes!' I said. 'And if we go to the little church by the river—will you be able to walk that far?' asked Villant. 'But of course I will,' I said. 'And what if we go, let's say, to the forest, Gere, and walk all day through the forest? What then?' 'I'm not afraid, Villant, when I'm with you,' I told him. And Villant's eyes changed. When I looked into his eyes his whole face had changed. 'Well, Gere,' said Villant, 'we can go wherever we like. Tell me, my friend, who can do anything to stop us?' I didn't answer because there was a strange look in Villant's eyes. Then Villant said, 'Tell me, Gere, I've got the right to go walking where I like, don't I? I'm telling you, Gere, that'll be quite a day—when the two of us go walking down the streets of the village.' "

The room was filled with the sound of Villant's mother sobbing. She was choking with the tears. Gere turned around to look at her and noticed that his mother was also crying. She was looking up, and the tears were trickling down her cheeks. The magistrate said nothing. He let Villant's mother cry. As he gazed at her, Gere slowly began to discover Villant's face in hers. She had Villant's forehead, and her hair was the same as his.

"Then Villant stood in front of the mirror," continued Gere, "and he said to me, 'I've got a very lovely face, you know. Who knows if you'll remember me for long, dear child! If you'll remember me forever?' said Villant. 'I will remember you,' I told him. 'I know you will,' said Villant, 'and I was fool enough to doubt it.' "

Villant's mother broke out again into loud sobs. For a long time nobody said anything. Then one of the peasants stood up and said, "Comrade Magistrate, I suggest we send the child home. Go home, sonny. Go home and play."

Gere rose and picked up his shoes, eager to run outside.

"Wait, comrades," said the magistrate. "You too, Gere. Wait, my boy—don't be afraid. After all, comrades, that's what we came here for. A case of death has been reported here, and it's also been reported that the circumstances are suspicious. There is reason to believe that it isn't a case of accidental death, but of murder. And I've been ordered to hold an inquiry."

The peasant who had told Gere to go home now stood up and began to speak. "The man you want is Done Trupac, Comrade Magistrate. We know him well. He just can't live without kicking up some sort of scandal. That's the way he is, and you shouldn't trust him any more. It'd be far better if Done Trupac wasn't in our village," said the peasant, and he sat down.

The magistrate mopped his brow with the handkerchief made of parachute silk. "Come now, Gere; try to remember what happened after that."

Silence reigned in the room again. Gere was playing with his fingers thoughtfully. " 'But you don't need to remember me any more, Gere,' Villant said. 'Why the devil should you remember me, my little friend? You know what?' Villant said. And he took my hand. 'I'll give you the little box of toys,' he said. 'You keep the box here, Villant,' I told him, 'and I'll come over here to play.' 'Gere,' he said, 'it's a shame for me to have toys like that at home. They're for little children. I want you to take the box home with you.' 'All right, Villant,' I said, 'I'll take it with me when I go home.' So now the box is with me. It's a little yellow box full of American toys. But one of the fret saws is broken, the one which Boro broke."

"It broke itself," Boro interrupted.

"So you went home straight away, Gere?" asked the magistrate.

"No," said Gere. "Villant first told me he wanted to read me something that evening. 'All right, Villant,' I said. 'Read aloud if you like.' 'I'm not going to read at all, Gere,' said Villant. 'This reading is no help to either of us. Let's talk about something instead,' he told me. 'Everything will be fine, Gere,' Villant told me. 'I won't let anything happen as long as I have you. And don't you forget, Gere, in a few days you and I will take a walk through the village.' 'We'll go down to the meadow as well,' I said. 'Yes,' said Villant, 'we'll go there as well.' Then my mother and father came. My mother said 'Good evening,' and my father said, 'My goodness, Villant, you look as fit as a boxer.' 'Yes,' said Villant, 'just like John Lucas.' My father was silent. Villant smiled and whispered to me, 'He's a boxer.' 'Daddy,' I said, 'John Lucas is a boxer.' Villant smiled again and said, 'That's not the way to say it, Gere,' and then he told me how to say the name. Then Villant asked where his mother had gone, and my mother told him that she was staying with Aunt

Famia. That was all she said. 'Well, Villant,' said my father, 'we're going now.' 'All right,' said Villant. 'I want to give Gere the box of toys. I feel ashamed to be playing with these toys.' I took the box and we set off. Mummy and Daddy said goodbye to Villant. The next day my father told me to get out of bed because we were going to the village where Granny Filipica lives. 'Gere,' he said to me, 'we'll go on horseback, you and me.' "

"And then what happened?" The magistrate turned to the peasants.

One of the peasants looked at Villant's mother and began to speak. "After they had left, Villant went up to the granary in his wheel chair. He tore two boards off the railing and threw himself over the edge in his chair—straight down onto the cobbles. When his mother returned, she found him dead. All the young people came to his funeral. We were all very fond of Villant, because even when he was only a very young boy he used to be the best boxer in all four villages. He was our best boxer. . . ," the peasant's voice trailed off. He wanted to add something more but did not know what to say.

The magistrate turned to the clerk of the records. "Write *Ad acta* across the records so that there can be no mistake. As you have heard for yourselves, comrades, there can be no question of murder whatsoever," he said to the peasants. "You may go home now. I must leave at once, while there's still time."

The peasants began to jostle their way out through the door.

"Oh, I nearly forgot," said the judge. "There's just one more thing. The Town Council told me to remind you to hold a meeting and discuss the running of the farms. We must submit a report as soon as possible."

The Shirt

"There were three of us, my little friend," he said. Everybody was "little" to him, even I, although he was a head shorter than I was. "There were three of us, my little friend," he repeated. "In the morning when we were hungry, or when we wanted to attract Lilla's attention—she was the landlady's maid—we used to smash stacks of ridge-tiles with our bare hands. You don't believe me? Ah, I used to break up to ten of them at a time with my right hand. Chopped them in half, I did. And the little maid—she used to laugh her head off and clap her hands with delight. She must have realized why we broke them. Do you think she'd ever tell the boss? Not bloody likely! She enjoyed it, my little friend, as much as we did.

"But, you know, if you do something too often it gets boring. We got bored with breaking the tiles. We got bored with her too. Perhaps because she got herself involved with a lover. No, no, the lucky man wasn't one of us. It was the watchman out on the site; she got involved with him, and they gave her the sack. They were caught in the act—

Srbo Ivanovski, like so many of the writers of short stories in Macedonia, is also known as a poet—in fact, better known as a poet. He was born in 1928 in Štip, the largest town in eastern Macedonia, was graduated from the Faculty of Philosophy in Skopje, and now works at Skopje Radio–TV. Ivanovski has been a figure of some literary importance since the early 1950s, having published in the last twenty years some eight collections of poetry, a collection of short stories, and a novel.

This brief story concerns the *pečalbari*, the itinerant Macedonian masons and craftsmen who, almost without interruption throughout this century, have wandered far from home during the working season. The *pečalbari* frequently travel in groups and leave their families behind in their wanderings in search of work.

the whole hog, you understand? And so we were left alone. All alone with that endless monotony. Everything had already been done. But the season went on, just like now.

"September was passing, and every new day was lovelier than the last, but it dawned just for the ridge-tiles. During those first few days we talked of nothing but home. One always talks about home in September. Then these conversations also dried up. There was no longer anything left to talk about. All we could find to do was to go and buy presents. And so we went to town. Every day a few of us would. We would buy shoes or trousers for the winter. Some of the men would buy dresses for their wives. When you come back after working abroad, you have to take something home. Yes, my little friend, that's the way we lived. And as for the ridge-tiles—well, nothing more need be said. They were eternally with us, although we did our damnedest to forget them. And we're still trying," he gave a cunning smile.

"Then, in the midst of all this boredom, it happened. It was late in the afternoon when Pandei came running towards us. He was all red and excited.

" 'It's gone,' he said. 'The shirt I bought yesterday—it's gone. It was a lovely shirt. White, with a stiff collar and double cuffs. We spent a whole hour bargaining for it with the shop assistant.'

" 'Go and look for it,' I said. 'Who would take it?'

"He went away and closed all the doors. Then he walked through all the rooms, one after the other. He said that there was no other way of finding it, and that somebody must surely have taken it. Somebody must have stolen it. We stood out in the yard watching him going in and coming out of the rooms. We kept our hands in our pockets and didn't say a word. At times like this it's very hard to talk. Very hard. You know, each of us felt a little bit like a thief, but at the same time we were offended. I don't know what words everyone had in his mouth but I know full well that even if it had turned out to be my worst enemy who took it,

I was ready to do absolutely anything just as long as it wasn't found.

"But he found it. He brought it out hooked onto his finger, and when he appeared the tension that had been building up in our chests suddenly dissolved. We all let out that bitter air that had been pent up inside us. He came over to us. He was looking for someone. Then he stopped and turned towards the bricklayer, who was sitting on a low stone.

" 'You,' he said.

"The bricklayer did not lift his eyes. He didn't move. But everyone began to mutter.

" 'You,' Pandei said again. 'You stole it.'

" 'He's just come back from town,' said the gray-haired watchman. 'He only arrived a few moments ago.' The bricklayer did not move. He stared straight ahead, but it seemed like he was looking backwards into himself.

" 'It was on his bed,' said Pandei, and then he shouted 'Speak!' at the bricklayer. 'Speak!' he shouted. And then he said, 'You want me to stroke you a little, huh? And then we'll talk?' But the bricklayer didn't even look at him. Then Pandei went and got a rope. But still the bricklayer was silent. He didn't do anything when they bound his hands and threw the other end of the rope over a beam. He stood up straight, his hands above his head, but his eyes were empty. Indifferent. He had no shoes on, and his pants were torn, and his legs were all dusty. And he had no shirt and couldn't even button his jacket.

"It wasn't very pretty. Everybody was staring at him from all sides, and the eyes were all very sharp. Then they started cursing him, those words which could hardly wait to be spoken. Maybe it would have all ended differently if only he had said something. But he just stood there, tall and straight, his hands stretched high above his head by the rope thrown over the beam. People walked around him, but they weren't very satisfied. They began to laugh within themselves both at the shirt and at this thief who had been so stupid.

"Then the watchman said, 'Well, it's his first time, isn't it?' And they untied him. He just sat down on the same stone, staring into the night. There weren't lights in the dormitory; all had small lamps. But he didn't light his lamp that night. When we went in to bed he stayed outside in the yard by himself. Nobody wanted to go near him. He seemed to have withdrawn completely into himself and just sat there, silent, staring into the dark. No, he didn't seem mad, but all the same—it was strange. Maybe somebody should have stayed with him all night to keep an eye on him. But who would want to sit up all night?

"The next morning, before the bell rang, Pandei woke me, shouting that his shirt had been stolen again.

"He plonked his big foot on my bed and stood there looking at the wall for a minute. Then he bent down and looked under his own to see if it hadn't fallen. But the shirt wasn't on the floor either. He went out, and then he came back. 'His bed hasn't been slept in,' he said. 'He probably wanted to make me pay for what happened yesterday. What did I do to him? Why did he have to get so mad? I'm the one who should be mad. I could have called the cops!'

"A little while later they found him. Dead. He was hanging from the same rope that they had tied him with the day before. But now it was stretched tight around his neck. And his eyes still had that funny look, staring out and in at the same time. It was the first time we'd seen him wearing a shirt—Pandei's lovely white shirt with the stiff collar.

"They cut down the rope. But it was too late. Far too late. Then somebody went into town, and around midday a car pulled up in the yard. First the boss got out. Two men followed him. They walked slowly, like at a funeral. One of the men asked whether anybody had touched anything when we had found him in the stable, but the watchman said, 'We just cut him down.' Then the boss's man stared for a long time at the yellow body on the ground and said that maybe it was suicide.

"The other man agreed. The boss nodded too. So did we.

But when we left the stable we suddenly felt fagged out. It was like part of our lives had been left behind with that body. It's the guilty feeling that tortures you the most, my little friend. And every one of us felt guilty then. We all felt like we were responsible. Weren't we part of him, inside him? Didn't we hang him? Didn't we tie the rope? But it wasn't the body itself that was bothering us. A body is of no more use when a man dies.

"We didn't talk to each other. Each man seemed to fear his neighbor. Everyone else's eyes seemed too dark. We went through the wide yard trying hard not to look at the empty beam above the door, but we could all see that brick-layer with his hands stretched above his head. He could have cut clean through us with that look of his that went both ways.

"Two days later the boss came again. He said that everything had been fixed up about the bricklayer. He said that he wasn't going to question anybody, that everything was perfectly clear. He said that the bricklayer had killed himself because he had gambled away all his money in town that day. All the money he had earned that summer. He had lost it all—right down to the last dinar. And he had worked a long time for that money; he had worked all summer.

"The boss was telling the truth. Although I didn't like him, I knew he was telling the truth. He had lost his money on that colored wheel and those white balls that jump over the colored numbers when the wheel spins round. Perhaps that was why he had been so tight-mouthed when he was standing there with his hands stretched above his head. The Devil only knows."

"And the shirt?" I asked.

"The shirt, my little friend? Pandei took it off him as soon as we had cut down the rope. The bricklayer didn't need it. You know, people come into this world without a shirt, so they might as well leave without one."

BOŽIN PAVLOVSKI

Border Incident

Original title, *The Man Who Panicked at the Border*

The man was walking along the border.

On either side of the border, running down both sides of the dividing space, were hedges of tall, ancient shrubbery. The man continued walking without altering his pace. Every morning this man followed the same path. He had noticed that the shrubbery was putting out weary shoots in defense against the times and the oppressive humidity, and day by day it came to remind him more and more of defeated soldiers. The grass in front of the shrubs was light green, because only a very few people ever walked on it. In the distance the grass took on a darker shade; it stretched as far as the eye could see to a point where the old undergrowth on both sides of the border seemed to tangle together in a forest. There in the distance the light fell like the green and yellow flowers which soak up the sun. At that point the path seemed to disappear.

The man had often gazed at all this, and so it was that on his walks he had assumed that there were no settlements on either side of the border. The wood was enlivened by wild

---

Božin Pavlovski was born in the village of Žvan, near Bitola, in 1942. He attended school in Bitola, studied at the university in Skopje, and began his writing career there as a journalist. Now he lives in Skopje, where he is a director of Misla, a leading Macedonian publishing house.

Pavlovski's stories have been collected in Macedonia under the title of *The Fantasts* (1967), and another collection, translated into Italian, has appeared under the title of *L'ombra di Radovan*. He has also written two novels: *Love Song* (1964) and the recent two-part novel of the rootless and disoriented "little" people in modern Skopje, *Miladin from China* (1967 and 1968).

animals and small birds that flew in from the nearest archipelago when the larger birds of the north departed for
the great plains. For him no other world could exist, and
he looked at the blue sky and the green wood. But the
murmuring streams did not find an answering echo in his
soul, the undergrowth rebuffed him, and everything foun-
dered before the emptiness of his life. He longed to die or
to disintegrate. He could, in fact, have felt the beauty of
spring, for the winds from the Aegean, the Mediterranean,
and the Ionian seas constantly blew across the border and
dried the drops of moisture with which the shrubs nourished
their flowers in the very first days of March. But he was
constantly preoccupied with his search and had no time for
nature. Yet now the fresh, greening spring spread around
him on all sides and flooded his senses. Above his head hung
a strange sky from which songs poured down, a sky in
which there were no clouds, white or black, a sky which had
distanced itself from the earth with its blueness. The man
was interested in the secrets of the sky for a very simple
reason; he was surrounded by untouched nature. And so he
lingered by this old, tired shrubbery from which a stray
gust of wind could shake the water left behind by the rain.

As he walked, like a poet through a field, he slowly drew
closer to two white watchtowers surrounded by walls and
various strange objects. There, beside the watchtowers and
the army quarters, he lost what little curiosity he had. He
was ready, if necessary, to feel fright, to put his hands up
if he had to, and to surrender. Between the soldiers and
the beginning of his path, somewhere in the background,
he had left behind that dark forest full of various greens.
He was once again aware of the fact of the duality of a
border, of the simultaneity of two countries; he was walking along the one side, and along the other a transparent
light was filling the grass. But then he did not even have
the right to peer over the edge of the border. For two
soldiers, one in olive-green uniform and the other in a

forest-green shirt, were standing in front of the watchtowers of their respective countries, their rifles slung over
their shoulders.

The man stared abstractedly at the soldiers; both silently
watched him out of the corners of their eyes and pretended
not to notice him. Then each soldier shifted his glance and
looked to his own side. They could have driven away any
creature they liked from that path of his, but they felt
sorry for the man who behaved so quietly, almost as though
he did not exist. He was standing before them and sur-
rendering himself to them. The forest and the streams all
belonged to him, all spoke his language, and yet he was
powerless. Instead of telling them that he was only looking
for a woman and that the rest of the world did not interest
him in the least, he held his peace. The soldiers might still
have wondered why he did not come to his senses and seek
his happiness and his rest somewhere far away from the
border where life has a genuinely attractive color, where life
is safe. But he was obviously invoking some privilege by
which he was able to pass in front of the soldiers who
usually asked no questions, for he went up beside the hedge
just across from them and sat down on the grass and stared
long and hard at the ground. Nature around him went on
with its same easy, primal existence. The soldiers waited
quietly for the change of guard. The little birds from the
islands of the south went on stripping the bark from the
shrubs, and somewhere, in the distance, the noise of engines
and passing cars could be heard. The man fell into a strange
somnolence, moving the muscles of his arms toward the two
countries that lay before his eyes. Occasionally he flung a
handful of earth and pebbles in the direction of one of the
countries, but later he would regret his action and would
look across to the other country to see if he had been
noticed.

"That's not allowed," shouted one of the soldiers.

"That's not allowed," the other soldier would add somewhat later.

The man's fingers trembled; he looked sadly toward them. But it seemed to him that nobody had said anything. Then he brushed the soil from his fingers on his old yellow coat, the kind that is worn in countries that border on the northern seas. Then the soldier on the opposite side, in the opposite country, looked angrily at the place where the pebbles and clods of earth had fallen somewhere in the grass. Near where the pebbles fell a dog barked, although none had the courage to appear on the grass. Perhaps it gave the man pleasure to have provoked something, to have angered something in another country.

Then there were also moments when he felt that it was because of an overpowering thirst that he had come to this region, that he had returned here to touch objects of reality, the unfeeling symbols of his love. Or, perhaps, he would at the same time feel astonished at his own boldness in remaining on the very edge of the border when not even birds or insects dared to move. In fact he constantly felt a small kernel of fear growing in him, fear that he might be driven back inland or that the soldiers might capture him and lock him up in the house by the watchtower.

Then, when the March sun reached its zenith, the man crawled into the shade of the undergrowth. The soldiers by now were looking impatiently on all sides. They could not care less what he did, for they had grown used to seeing him every day. What interested them was when the next watch would be coming to relieve them.

At about this hour an old, gray-haired woman used to appear on the other side of the border in the other country. She never sat down, but spent her time collecting various grasses and vines. She adhered most assiduously to the habit of greeting the man who was sitting in the shade and, no doubt out of spite, behaved toward the soldiers as though they did not exist. She was always singing a quiet song from a distant place, a song of flood tides and ebb tides, of sponge divers who disappear in the depths of the sea. Her accent as she sang was that of the people from the peninsula. This singing always raised the man's spirits, and courteously he stood up and listened with great attention, leaning against a tree. The soldiers, who had still not been relieved, would be growing impatient now, and they would shrug their shoulders uncomprehendingly. Yet they were surprised at the silent and mutual respect and understanding that existed between the man and woman. The woman, with that same song on her lips, often smoothed her hair sorrowfully and came toward the border; then the man, listening intently to her song, would try to hide his dirty, black, worn-out shirt.

"Good afternoon," he said.

"Good afternoon," the woman answered. "I'm gathering plants."

"I'm waiting here for my family," he replied.

"I saw my husband off from here when he went away," the woman continued.

"No matter where they went, they'll come back here," he said.

"Of course they will. My husband will return also."

Convinced of the truth of their words, they both looked down at the ground. The woman continued her song about the distant seas and the sponge divers, and the man, sitting down in the shade of the tree, picked up pebbles and tossed them into the grass of the country on the opposite side, where the dog was barking. Time passed quite naturally. The soldiers quietly guarded their watchtowers and waited to be relieved. Occasionally the man felt the desire to gaze out at the tangled forest of darkness where the border was concealed by the shrubbery. The gray-haired woman, her basket full of grasses and vines, then disappeared into the depths of the other country. Then a high bugle note sounded from the building by the watchtower, and the next squad of guards silently took over the watch. The dog that had been barking in the other country came out onto the small grass clearing with young children bounding after him. They did not notice that nearby a man was sitting in the undergrowth.

The children frolicked in full view of the man and paid no attention to him whatsoever. Now he was forced to recognize that there was some kind of settlement near the border. He expected the children to ask what he was doing there, sitting in the shade, and he was thinking of leaving, but then he noticed that the children spoke a different language. They scrambled up to the edge of the border and pulled the first spring flowers, which had sprung up in the heat of the March sun and the humid warmth of the Mediterranean air. Then they scurried back across the grass to the place where the wretched dog was still barking.

Then he remembered that a great festival day was approaching, a day to be more important than any he had known since childhood, for it was the day destined for his meeting. It almost seemed as though some day soon now the gentle spring rain might again fall, that rain which was always so beautiful, rich, and warm. And the memory of another world of time stirred up a feeling of restlessness in his soul.

He watched the new soldiers on the other side. They were particularly ugly, with their faces raised toward the sky. Not a drop of water fell, but they did not want to look at one another. The man at last began to fear that those soldiers might be so inhuman as to force him back along one of the roads leading inland. However, they did nothing; their guns were held silent and straight, cutting the clear air; their uniforms were clean and new. Slightly saddened by all this, the man thought of rising and of pacing backward and forward through a fresh day in an imagined place. Here and there a few wild birds sped past, but their revels meant nothing to him, confined as he was within the space of his imagined life.

It was only later that he became aware, from behind him, of the distant voices of other schoolchildren with books under their arms, leaping and shouting through the far undergrowth. At the other end of the field, somewhere far away, there must surely have been a school and another settlement. He stood up among the bushes and stretched his stiff limbs. For a moment he thought he could hear the gray-haired woman's song, the song that told of battles on the southern shores, of sponge divers and migrant laborers. The man looked over at the opposite side, but he saw nothing, only the waving grass, and he heard nothing, only the sound of children's cries mixed with the barking of the dog. There were still the soldiers with their paunches thrust out and the schoolchildren enjoying the true beauty of the new spring.

"My son will be coming," shouted the man.

"Some nutty old man," said one of the children close by.

A soldier in the olive-colored uniform turned his attention toward the voices and thought of warning the children that all play was forbidden near the border. Before he did so, however, the youngsters had disappeared into the thick cover of the forest. The man was once again left alone beside his flowering shrub.

Now the new soldiers had noticed him and were observing him with curiosity. It was a wonderful afternoon, drenched with warmth, sunlight, and the smell of sea spray; the sea was surely sparkling beyond the nearest bush-covered hills. The smell of dinner cooking in fat spilled out of the building by the watchtower guarded by the soldiers in olive uniforms, while from the other side of the border, from the other country, came the sad strains of folk music. The soldiers were unable to resist the rhythm and each began moving slightly in their places. But they kept firm holds on their rifles.

"What are you waiting here for?" asked one of the soldiers in a steely voice.

"For my family, of course," said the man.

The soldier took his gun in one hand, and turned toward the man. The man stepped back, frightened, trying to find the words to explain that he had been born in this place long ago, that he had grown up on both sides of the border because in those days there had been no soldiers, no watchtowers, no border, that after he had grown up he had become a soldier, that he had been on the losing side, had abandoned his family, and had sailed far, far away to the shores of the northern seas and later to the lands of the east, toward Asia. Both soldiers listened attentively, nodding their heads. In the forests the wild little sea birds were pecking at the bushes, and on a road somewhere far out across the fields came the sound of an engine and a heavy truck passing. The sun was setting directly into the thick green forest in the interior of the country to the north.

"We were supposed to meet here," said the man.

"Maybe it's too late," said one of the soldiers.

The soldier in the olive uniform let his head drop, slung his rifle onto the other shoulder, and turned to the soldier in the forest-green shirt. This soldier then looked back toward his country, from where one could hear the plangent sounds of folk music. The man began to approach the watchtower on his side, but the soldier advised him to keep well clear of the military buildings. The air was full of the smell of wild animals, the evening was drawing on, and soon the sun would disappear behind the hill. Sad and lonely, the man set off toward the interior of his country, again making his way along the edge of the border and toward the thick forest. He lingered on the way like a wild beast; his eyes were smarting both from what he had seen and from what he had not seen. Desperately unhappy, he vanished in the forest and left the soldiers to guard the border between the two countries. It had been a strange journey, a journey without a starting point, a wandering from one place to another, in search of a woman who was now the head of his family. This had been a day in which he had met only a shadow resembling something of the past. There had been other days as well when his search had been in vain.

*   *   *   *

Some days later, when he returned along the same path,
he was full of unusual desires. Although he had not heard
the sounds of the wild animals that roamed the forest, he
was, all the same, strangely disturbed by the cries of delight
that broke from the small birds that flew in from the open
sea, from some archipelago. Filled with delight by the
greenery, he continued walking along the border. It was the
warm, bright time of the spring, there were no clouds in
the sky, gray or white, and all was clean and quiet in the
space between the two countries. Both soldiers were at their
posts. The air was again alive with the provocative smell
of food and the plangent sound of music. He reached the
watchtower on his side, sat across from its walls, and began
to talk shyly to the soldier. He had been fed on the air of
these coastal parts and had not been able to stand it up
there in the north; he couldn't take the rush of life in the
big city, where he had no relatives and where he did not
wish to die. He felt that fate had drawn him back, he told
the soldier; he was sure that his wishes would soon be ful-
filled. He was crazy with impatience, but he would have to
go on waiting. The soldier on the opposite side clacked his
tongue to avoid overhearing the conversation, but the man
deliberately turned his face toward him.

"You aren't allowed to talk to me," said the soldier.

The man had forgotten this. He blushed in confusion and,
catching his breath, turned away shamefacedly into the ancient, weary shrubbery. He almost burst into tears, and he
was quite ready to fall asleep or to die. Soon, as always, his
journey to the far side of the country would have to begin.
However, soon the old gray-haired woman came, and she
was singing a new song about ikon painters, about the infidels from Corinth and about some well-known heroes
from the peninsula. She filled her wicker basket with grasses
and vines. As she worked, she sang a song about sea battles,
about sponge divers. But she was hurrying, as though she

had some far more important work to do. When she reached
the border her greeting revealed her empty mouth and bare
gums. The man was happy. He did not try to hide his shirt
now. He stood up beside the tree and made a little bow to
the woman. But he was unable to say a word. He knew that
with one word alone he might change many things and that
then he might no longer be weak. Moreover, his spirit was
in such a state that he was no longer sure of himself.

"I'm still waiting!" shouted the woman as she touched
her grasses and vines.

"It's not allowed! It's not allowed!" shouted the soldiers
from the watchtowers.

The woman, still with a song on her lips, went off in
search of more grasses, and the man sat down again in the
shade of the old shrubbery. Far away, in front of him, he
could see all the familiar colors of nature: the thick forest
with its trees jutting up between earth and sun, the sweep
of the boundary space, which vanished into infinity. Beyond the boundary, in the other country, a sound could be
heard; now a local band was strolling among the hills to
announce the start of wedding celebrations. The dog was
not barking, although the man now was constantly flinging
small stones and clods of earth. Behind him, as usual, he
could tell that engines were running and that cars were passing. The soldiers at their posts were beginning to look impatiently at the watchtowers and buildings in the hope of
being relieved by the next watch. Nothing happened. The
warmth of March besieged the border, and soon the air
was stirred by a sea breeze.

"I've met you somewhere before," shouted the soldier
in the olive uniform.

"In Tashkent most likely," shouted the man from far
away.

"No," said the soldier, "I've never been to Tashkent."

"In Asia then," shouted the man.

"Maybe," answered the soldier, "but I don't even know
where Asia is."

The man let his head drop again unhappily and settled back to his place among the bushes. The soldiers, proud and erect, turned to one another in common sympathy with the man. Not even God himself could have known what caused this misery. Now the man was quite ready to go again through the forest of sad, old shrubs overgrown with moss, and to weep as he went, but somehow he felt that it was better to wait. The ground before him was covered with that same dusty grass which reminded him of a time that had once been, here on this land. In those past times the soldiers had been quite different from these now, and the forest had long since healed the wounds those other soldiers had inflicted upon it. The man assumed that the gray-haired woman must have survived those times of hand-to-hand fighting. However, the woman was no longer there on the other side of the border. In the grass in the other country the same dog was barking and behind him wedding music still spilled into the air. Some young man was getting married to a pale-faced girl. He could imagine the girl floating in the wind along the current of moist air flowing in from the sea.

The man looked like an alien, for he had come from alien lands to participate in the burial of his younger days, days that had been long before the war, which had begun so far back now in time. As he wiped the sweat from his face he felt again the smell of the sea, which was surely sparkling somewhere close by, near the jagged rocks. Then the children, followed by the barking of the dog, came darting excitedly out on the grass and played again their eternal game beside the shrubbery in the other country. They were running and shouting in some strange, incomprehensible language, but at times they looked directly into the man's eyes. Behind them he caught sight of the gray-haired woman; now she was running, not like the children, but toward him, straight across the grass. She was not singing about archipelagos from which the small birds of prey flew, nor was she singing about the sponge divers whom the sea had swallowed; she was wailing in his mother tongue as she ran.

The soldiers did not know what to make of this, so they motioned with their guns at her and watched helplessly to see whether the man who wanted to cross the border would show himself. There was a strange sense of emptiness and solitude such as is always felt at times of great excitement. How dully that emptiness echoed in the man! Like rarefied air, like an unexpected meeting, and like time delayed.

"You are my husband!" shouted the woman across the space. She was still running toward him.

"It isn't true!" he shouted back. "She doesn't look at all like you."

"I am your wife!" the woman cried as she approached.

The children stopped playing, the dog sat down among them like a friend. It was warm. Those were the first days of March. The man was completely taken aback. He bowed his head and began to search the past, the past that had drawn him back from so far away, even the northern seas. The soldiers were shouting. They were holding their guns at the ready and were praying that nothing would happen, that the woman would turn back. The soldier in the forest-green shirt looked behind him toward the place from which the wedding music could be heard clearly now. The air was slowly filling with the pleasant smell of food escaping from the building beside the watchtower, and the air gradually freshened as the humid heat began to ease off in the first cool of afternoon. The woman ran right across the border. The soldiers fired their rifles. She fell.

"You've killed her!" the man shouted. Now he rose and approached the border station.

"You panicked!" one of the soldiers said to the other.

Then both soldiers lowered their rifles, and although they belonged to different countries, they exchanged looks of shamed understanding. The children stood still and covered their ears with their fingers. Now, however, the man's love began to grow. He no longer felt poor and wretched. He would have preferred to die at once or to be destroyed with shame rather than to hear himself deny once more the bond between himself and that unfortunate woman. At this moment his love seemed to sweep through him; it overcame him; it grew so powerful that it encompassed all this space around the border and all the greenery as well. And still he sought some small trace of life from the woman lying at a distance on the grass.

As she was lying there, suddenly altered, he felt a sense of disgust with the realization that his lost world had its own place. Meanwhile, the soldiers shrugged their shoulders and wept. The sky, the forest, and the stream meant nothing to them, but they represented an entire youth to him. He began to move toward her. He took shorter and shorter steps. Then the soldiers would no longer permit him to approach the woman who, only a short while ago, had been singing songs about the seas, about the infidels from Corinth, about the sponge divers who returned or who did not return from the shores of Arabia. For a moment the distant shouts of children could be heard from behind him in the forest. These he had heard the day before. In front of him all was pale and silent, although in the distance the sound of the wedding celebrations could still be heard. The soldier in the olive uniform remained at his post while the other hurried into the watchtower to report that a woman had been accidentally shot. The man withdrew and sat down again under his bushes and turned his eyes toward the thick forest of tired, sad trees that, in the distance, took on a lively color in the sunlight.

Then three soldiers came out of the watchtower in the other country; they intended to carry away the woman's body. The children and the dog were gone. Along the border the soldier again stood with his rifle raised. But then the woman stood up, carefully shook the dirt from her dress and, without paying any attention to the three soldiers, turned toward the man.

"I knew you were a coward."

"But my wife did not have gray hair," he answered in self-justification.

"Of course," said the woman. "I just wanted to test you."

"Didn't I tell you something would happen?" said the man.

"But I wanted to make you happy," she replied.

"And you have hurt me very much," said the man.

The woman was no longer listening. She picked up her wicker basket and, favoring one leg, made her way back through the forest. The man stood up and cupped his hands to his mouth, as though he were about to shout something after her. The three soldiers walked along beside the woman and asked her to let them help her. The old shrubbery wove a thick cover around them, and the air became humid again.

"My love for her would have had no substance," the man muttered in his own defense. "My life has been changed."

Then he himself explained to the soldier that he now felt only the insignificant weight of his own being, that his life could be seen in the symbol of the bird of the wind and that he had come home to his birthplace in the south only to die. His words conjured up a time that had passed, long before the soldiers had come to those parts. It had been exceedingly painful for him to stay by the border, and soon, he said, he would return to the northern seas. There was no point in his waiting by the watchtower any longer, he explained to the soldier confidentially, but the soldier answered that even if he had wanted to stay, he would still have to have been driven away. In the end the old man admitted that he had simply come to see his homeland, and that was all.

"That woman's a tramp," he whispered to the soldier. "She was all set to make a slave of me."

"You've no idea what's going on," answered the soldier. "She's all alone, just like you." The soldier laughed a little. He could hear the sound of the wedding music; it cut right through the air.

Once again the man heard the sound of the woman's voice, singing about some fisherman lost in the waters of the

Ionian Sea, and about the infidels of Corinth, and it seemed that he still felt the need to be there after all, perhaps beside her. The reality that moved his spirit was, he felt, quite different from the dream with which he had come to the border. But that same dream had shaped the fate of many people.

The Typewriter

"Take one of the typewriters," they told him. "Nobody minds if you borrow one for a couple of days. After all, if you already know in your mind what you want to say, then you just have to sit down at the typewriter and knock it off. Come on! Courage, man! You've got it all straightened out upstairs, haven't you? Well then, the rest is a pushover."

He spent a long time going from one office to another in search of a suitable typewriter, but none of them was to his liking. They were either too cumbersome, or too heavy to the touch, or of an appearance he was sure would never harmonize with his personality. At all events, not one of these typewriters suited him, not one of them was appropriate to the quality of the ideas which were to be typed upon it. He was aware that the choice of typewriter might turn out to be of vital importance from the very moment he began to type; every part of the machine with which he failed to familiarize himself beforehand might easily spring a surprise on him when he began typing, and this might stop

---

Bogomil Gjuzel is the writer of the young generation who has, perhaps, done as much as any man living to bring Macedonian literature to the attention of a wider audience. Gjuzel was born in Čačak in 1939 and was educated at the University of Skopje, taking his degree in English literature. He also studied at the University of Edinburgh.

His first reputation as a writer was made with his poetry, which has been collected in several volumes, the first, *Mead,* appearing in 1962. He has also written for the theatre (his play *Adam and Eve,* of 1970, achieved remarkable success) and for television. Gjuzel has produced several translations from English and French and is also respected as a literary critic. He is presently living in Skopje with his English wife and their daughter, having recently returned from a year at the International Writers' Workshop at the University of Iowa.

the movement of the words that darted through his mind with the speed of meteors, bearing the ideas he was about to set down.

This did not mean that the concept, the idea he wished to set down on paper, was weak simply because it was liable to vanish at the slightest shock; far from it. For some time now this idea had been growing inside him with undiminishing vigor; he had felt it rising within him like an unborn child inside its mother's womb. There were moments when it would overwhelm him completely, breaking out in every word, in every look, in every movement of his hands. At such times he was unable to keep his hands still, and he would nervously fumble with the buttons on his coat or thrust his hands in and out of his pockets. When these fits of nervousness overtook him, he would sometimes be driven to ask his hands, "Where, for Heaven's sake, where d'you want to go?" Even when he was not doing anything with his hands, that is, when he was not buttoning and unbuttoning his coat or thrusting them in his pockets, he would gaze at them; his fingers would be twitching slightly, whispering to one another. They were capable of doing absolutely anything just to conceal that central power which moved them.

He was convinced that in all this fumbling and rummaging, in all these movements, there was evidence of the energy of ideas, and that if all this energy could in some way be imprinted upon his surroundings, transferred to some object, there could be no doubt that in this imprint, in this object, there might be embodied his thought, his great idea. Inspired by this belief, he would sometimes start examining the buttons around which, a short while ago, his fingers had been curled. Or he would begin peering into the pockets in which, a short while ago, his hands had been thrust. Needless to say, these investigations never led to anything. He, of course, was no fingerprint expert. Perhaps there really were signs and imprints on his buttons and in his pockets, marks that might have meant something but that could not be seen with the naked eye.

Then they told him to get hold of a typewriter. This would at least give his fingers something to do, they said, and this would produce an impression, leave behind a sign which would contain in itself the entire content of his thought, so that whenever he read this mark he would be able to recall his thought and find gratification in it. Indeed, since other people would also be able to see what he had written, it might enable them to experience something of his ideas for themselves.

So, he spent a long time hunting for a typewriter, but he simply could not find one that suited him. He went round to all the offices in town. But everywhere the result was the same; he would always end up by telling himself, "No, this won't do, either; it has some levers and wheels that are quite unfamiliar to me." He began to despair of ever finding a typewriter that would live up to his very specific expectations. And he was desperate, because he certainly could not construct such a machine himself.

One day, however, as he was wandering aimlessly and dejectedly down the street, he came upon a friend. "I hear you're looking for a typewriter," the friend said. "I've got one at home, if you're interested. It's a very old one, I'm afraid, but if you like we can go round to my place and take a look at it; perhaps it will be what you want." They set off for the house. He went along, out of respect for an old friendship, since he had little hope of finding what he wanted. They arrived and climbed up to the attic where, from the darkest and dustiest corner, his friend pulled out a black object which he said was a typewriter. Once they had cleaned off the thick layer of dust that had accumulated, he could tell by the shape of the case alone that this was the very machine he had been looking for. They quickly opened the case. And there it was—the one and only typewriter worthy of his idea.

He recognized it right away. Yes, there could be no doubt about it; this was the right one. He examined it carefully, although he knew quite well there was no need to do so.

No matter how hard he tried, he would not have been able to find a single flaw, a single fault that might distort or interfere with the transmission of his idea. Indeed, it would have been far better were he to alter his idea to suit this all-too-perfect typewriter. This machine seemed to have been his language; the place of every tiny wheel and screw seemed familiar to him. "It's pretty old, I'm afraid," said his friend, not understanding the reason for the close examination. "It was left to me after my father died. One of the letters is broken, I think."

"That's nothing. It can easily be fixed. All that matters is that I've found the very machine I was looking for."

Now that he had finally found a typewriter that would serve his idea, and now that a perfectly harmonious and balanced relationship was to be established between his grand concept and the typewriter that would transmit it, there was nothing left for him to do but to carry the machine from his friend's house and take it to his own home. He wanted to take it home because he knew full well that, even if his friend's house were put entirely at his disposal and he were allowed to type away there to his heart's content, he would not be happy if his contact with the beloved object were to be qualified by the presence of a third person. This, clearly, would amount to the same as not having contact with the object at all.

Borrowing the machine would not be difficult. He simply had to take care not to offend anybody. This problem was, as the phrase goes, of a purely technical nature. For the next few days he never left his friend's side. He agreed with everything he said. No, he didn't get down on his knees before him. He just offered his friendly approval and embodied the virtue of good old Christian loyalty. In brief, what happened was that during a few days he brought their friendship to such a point of intimacy that he was finally able to request that he be allowed to take the machine home with him, without fear that his request might give offense.

So, one evening, when he felt he was ready (he wanted

everything to be worked out with mathematical certitude) he decided that the time was ripe to ask for the typewriter. He played his hand with great skill; his request was dropped casually into a most ordinary conversation as easily as if he were making an innocent remark about the weather. By so doing he avoided all possibility of a refusal. Although a more formal request might have appealed to his friend's vanity and brought a vague reply such as "We'll see" or "I'll have to think it over," a remark such as he had made, dropped with a certain off-hand nonchalance into a conversation in which many more momentous questions were being considered, could not allow of such an answer. Since the remark had been so casually introduced it could only be received in the same vein, with a nonchalant acceptance strengthened by an awareness that the minor request should now no longer complicate the already tortuous ramifications of their discussion.

While they were on their way to fetch the typewriter (yes, his friend had agreed to satisfy the request as quickly as possible and to give him the machine that very evening), he found it exceptionally difficult to maintain a normal discourse. However, they finally reached the house, and his friend entered and emerged shortly afterward, carrying the typewriter, which he handed over in its case, even with the keys (thank God I'm rid of it! One object less! Now perhaps my life will be fuller and richer). One of them made a last remark about the weather, and then they parted. Alone now in the dark with the precious burden of the typewriter in his hands, he was overwhelmed by what had happened to him.

The experience was so powerful that it seemed unreal. He had, of course, anticipated great happiness on finally finding a typewriter, but he had never imagined that the difference between having and not having could be so enormous, so sharply defined. One minute there was something undefined, something remote, so far away that it could only be conceived of in the mind, and the next there was the firm feel, the mass, the weight of that something which one could go on forever touching and stroking, something that was too real and close even for one's self. Suddenly, as though after a great catastrophe, all the surrounding realities seemed to disappear—streets, houses, trees, all seemed to have been carried away, never to return, and only he was left, a solitary castaway on a barren rock in the empty expanse of the sea.

He felt that now something had to happen to fill this void which surrounded him. Something had to happen outside of him as an answer to the happiness within him, as a counter to the cry of joy within him. And this counter to his happiness might be caused by anything. A small dust storm might break off a piece of the sky, an ordinary cough or sneeze might cause roof tiles to fall. So he would have to watch his step carefully. Now, for example, he would have to race across the street as fast as he could to avoid being caught unawares by a car suddenly appearing from around a corner. And then, when he reached the pavement on the other side, he would try to make his feet glide over the ground, because one false step might disturb the lovely machinery of the typewriter. How could he know? Anything might happen now. What if he stumbled over a loose paving stone? O Lord, all the little cogs and screws would be displaced within the typewriter as he fell, and afterwards nobody would know how to put them back into their proper places again.

But that was not all. No, that was not all. If the typewriter were to be smashed when he fell, then the entire idea he was carrying within him would also be destroyed, because it was now inseparably bound to the typewriter. Something has to happen, something has to happen, he repeated. But, strange to say, he had already covered a good deal of the way, and nothing had happened, despite the fact that thousands of possibilities had already arisen in that emptiness, that vacancy which was as barren and deserted as the world on the first day, where any signs of motion, any movement whatsoever, could become a primal event. No, nothing had happened yet, although he still expected the inevitable. He was still in one piece. Perhaps, after all, nothing had to happen. No, no (how naive of him), something had to happen and that . . . oh, no! right at the next crossing. Yes, now at last something had to happen, since a road cut right across his path and since there was no other choice, no detour he could make, no way in which he could avoid it. He clasped the typewriter under his arm so that he could be as close to it as possible when the inevitable fall occurred.

He looked up the street to see if any cars were coming. But what would happen if no cars came? What was about to happen could easily happen even if no cars appeared. He was, however, distinctly more assured when he gained the opposite pathway. Was not his luck remarkable, so great that it could save him from any catastrophe, despite the dangers lurking at every step? He was now confident that even if someone had been plotting mischief against him, his luck would see him through—that is, he, his idea, and his typewriter would come through intact and unchanged. After all, the fact that he had already covered so much of the way without mishap and was now standing in front of his own home surely indicated clearly that luck was on his side. Now his happiness would really be pure—now, when he opened the door, climbed the stairs, and locked himself in his room, where he would finally be alone and safe.

Just as he was opening the door, there was a creak. Something had to happen; something had to happen. Suddenly it dawned on him that the very fact that nothing had happened to him the whole way proved more firmly and conclusively than anything else that something would, after all, happen. He felt a voice repeating inside him, a voice he knew was true. Yes, something really will happen to you, and it will be far worse than you expect. So, he thought, it has to be. All right, but when? Where? He closed the door. Down here or up in his room? He climbed carefully up the stairs. Perhaps in his room. He went inside.

Surely there couldn't be anything wrong with the typewriter. He tried to open the case, but the key only clicked
loosely. The case remained locked. No, no, surely not. He
tried turning the key again, left, right, but as he turned
it in the lock there was no resistance. So, it was the typewriter after all. The case could not be opened. Could anything be more bitterly ironic? There he was at last in his
room, alone, with the only typewriter that answered his
needs, and this wretched case (which he could have smashed
to bits in a few minutes) was standing between them. The
case was of no value in itself, and yet he was obliged to
handle it with care to avoid damaging anything inside, to
avoid damaging the typewriter itself.

Suddenly, however, there was a click, and the case opened,
as though it had never had any intention of remaining per-
petually closed. It had been opened by one of those in-
voluntary movements without which we would long since
have ceased to exist. His hand, quite unwittingly, had
pressed the button which he had taken for a mere decoration. It seemed, then, that this was not the accident that
had been destined to occur, since the typewriter was now
open and ready for writing. What had not happened earlier
was now of no importance to him. He sat down, settled
himself in his chair, drew from the drawer a white sheet
of paper, rolled it into the carriage, and held his fingers
ready to strike the keyboard.

What now? Well, go on, start from the beginning! What
beginning? Well, from the starting point. Look, I know that
your concept and your idea are quite complete, that is,
there's no beginning and no end, but in order to set them
down on this piece of paper you have to begin to develop
them somehow. Come on now, you must begin somehow,
you can't type it all out simultaneously. It doesn't matter
how you start, just start! All right . . . he pressed down
one key, but it made no impression on the paper. Then he
remembered that they had told him to hit the keys, not

press them. Very well, then, he was going to hit them. So . . .
O – CLACK, N – CLACK, E – CLACK, N – CLACK, I – CLACK,
G – CLACK, H – CLACK, T – CLACK, I – CLACK, N – CLACK,
A – CLACK, P – CLACK, R – CLACK, I – CLACK, L – CLACK . . .

Hold on, hold on, something seems to have gone wrong;
there's something else setting up a disturbance between the
idea and the typewriter, and it gets bigger every time I hit
the keys. Look, it's already quite big, and it's present
throughout the room. I can feel its damp touch on my face.
Some third thing has come into this room. He began to
strain after his idea, but he felt it slipping further and
further away from him. Those marks he had made on the
paper, onenightinapril, meant nothing together, and when
he *HIT* the keys—oh, he wished all this typing could be
done without any *NOISE*. To make matters worse, somebody might *HEAR* what he was typing.

It was clear to him that he could not continue like this.
Every tap on the keys troubled him more; in the end the
noise might become so great that he would be forced outside. It was a good thing, after all, that he had stopped
typing in time.

This, then, was what was to happen. He cursed his luck.
He had everything he needed to set his ideas down: an open
typewriter, paper, fingers. But he could not possibly have
foreseen that in the very process of transforming his
thoughts into words he would have to put up with this
infernal clattering, which was so loud that it was driving
him to distraction. Now the machine itself lost its importance, not because he had ceased to be fond of it nor because
he wanted to hurl it through the window or smash it to bits.
No, far from it, his affection toward it was still warm; he
had spent far too much time in finding it to begin finding
fault now. But the typewriter, although it was in no way
to blame, had simply lost its significance and had been reduced to the level of many other things that were also in
some unfortunate way connected with his idea. There were

the things such as the buttons and pockets already mentioned. Now he would have to look after the typewriter,
and to feed it. It could not feed him.

He was, nevertheless, far from beaten. In the end, it was
a good thing that the inevitable had happened, had taken
a form (or a sound) so he could now recognize it. It simply
meant that his mind was not properly equipped to withstand the clattering of this machine. This did not necessarily
imply that he would be unable to endure when he found
himself confronted with a primitive sound, which would
certainly be produced by any other form of typing or writing—but with an ordinary pencil? Oh, why did he not think
of this before? That was the answer—a pencil! He immediately began to rummage through his drawer. He wasn't
going to write in ink; he thrust aside the pens. Oh, Lord,
how could I write with a pen when I know it is not the
whole pen, nib, barrel, and top that does the writing, but
only a thin thread of ink flowing out at the end. The same
goes for mechanical pencils with their flimsy bits of lead
that either fall out or break. No, no, I can't possibly write
with them, only with a proper wooden pencil. He finally
drew out a wooden pencil, strong lead firmly fixed from
one end to the other, a pencil he could hold firmly between
his fingers, a pencil that could not possibly break.

Then he took another sheet of paper and began to write:
one night in April a solitary lamp was burning . . . what
was the matter this time? Could he not even stand the sound
of a pencil scratching? At every sh-shh he gave a nervous
start, like a sparrow. Wait, let's see what I've written. Ugh,
nothing. What did I want, what's this meant to be? What
if . . . etc. He was deeply distressed. Even the whiteness of
the paper disturbed him, not so much because of the color—
that could be easily changed—to yellow, for example—but
because of the emptiness of the sheet.

It now seemed pointless for him to continue, since whenever he undertook the transmission of inner thought into

outer reality the undertaking always produced some by-product, something independent of him that he simply could not tolerate. It seemed incredible, but what had already happened was foredoomed. He was destined for silence.

The Strong, Hot Wind

I

Oh, God, how strong and hot this wind is. How cunningly it whips up the dust from the streets, flings it onto the rooftops and from there sends it scudding over the fields. The sky is dark blue with waiting. The fields are yellow and parched; the streets are the eyes of the sky. And all would be the same as it once was if the airplanes started machine-gunning this silence filled with the heat of the wind.

Oh, God, how strong and hot this wind is.

She was sitting in the half-dark room thinking back to that evening when the wind had beat like this before against the windowpanes. It had been a hot wind, too, that evening, but not an autumn wind. The dusk had been filled with the scent of greenery, the streets had been the eyes of the sky, and late that afternoon the airplanes had machine-gunned the silence. The hot wind had been the herald of waiting, and Smiljka had been sitting opposite her, facing away from the window. They had been thinking of the same thing, the same words had stuck in their throats, unuttered, and the same hope had lain in their hearts. Then Smiljka had stood up and turned toward the window, the pale light of the dying day clinging to her eyelashes.

"What a mad wind this is," Smiljka had said. "It's going

Branko Varošlija was born in the Kosovo in 1934 and educated at the Classical Grammar School and the Faculty of Philosophy at Skopje. He began writing as a schoolboy and has published his stories widely in periodicals, although they have yet to be collected. His one novel, *The Last Flight of the Migratory Bird* (1968), was well received by critics, however, and his plays are well known to Skopje audiences, both in the legitimate theatre and on television.

to ruin the flowers." When she moved away from the window, the light of the dying day was still lingering on her eyelashes.

She'll be going now, she had thought.

"He'll come back soon. I'm sure he will, aren't you?" Smiljka had asked.

"Yes," she had replied. "He'll come back." She'll be going now, she had thought. First she'll wander round the room, then she'll leave.

Smiljka had gazed into her eyes.

"Yes, he'll be back, I'm sure he'll be back. I can feel it inside me," she had said.

After Smiljka left she had watched her through the window as she cut quickly across the street to the gate of the house opposite. She had remained like that for a long time, staring at the road, feeling that she was alone with the wind and that out there where he was, on the flat lands of Srem, the hot wind would be blowing as it was at home and sighing with the whistle of bullets. And the two of them, she and Smiljka, waiting for him to come. . . . When he returned she would no longer be alone in the empty, voiceless room. And she had sensed with a pleasant certainty that he would come, just as she had sensed that the town would be liberated only a few days before the liberation took place.

"He will come," she had repeated aloud, sitting down on the couch so as to summon up more clearly the day of his arrival. She had pictured every detail of the scene. He would be there, and she and Smiljka. Then, without concentrating on anything in particular, she had listened to the wind, still hot and strong, blowing through the empty street.

Then the door had banged. She had stood up. No, it wasn't he, although the man was dressed, it seemed, in the same khaki clothes as her son.

It was that sad man with the wrinkled face who had told her in a trembling voice that her son had been killed and that he would be brought to her the next day.

All that night they had sobbed silently, inwardly, she

and Smiljka. And, outside, the wind, hot and strong, sobbed
with them. Smiljka's slender body had lain on the blanket.
She had held the girl's face in her hands, resting lifelessly in
her lap. Smiljka had sobbed her heart out and then, raising
her head slightly, had stammered out: "He will still come—
don't you feel that he will?"

She had not answered.

Outside the wind was sobbing.

                        *   *   *   *

She was standing beside the window. She wondered why,
whenever the wind blew and the darkness swallowed the
edges of the walls, her thoughts always reverted to the same
point. Why did she feel so sad and lonely whenever the
wind blew—the wind that always had to be so hot (was it
always hot?)—and the darkness swallowed the edges of
the walls, and only the street, like an emptiness within an
emptiness, cut a lonely path through the darkness? Was it
because so many years ago in that emptiness within an
emptiness, when she had been standing there by the window with the strong, young wind blowing outside, she had
seen him with Smiljka and had not been afraid that he
might be "spoilt"? She had felt both of them close to her
then, as if they were both her own and so close that the
spirit of youthful restlessness had begun again to burn in
her, too, like a fatal spark leaping out of the dying embers
of a fire. Was it because, when he had entered the room, un-
kempt and disheveled, and had sighed, "Oh, God, how
strong and hot this wind is," she had first repeated his
words to herself: "Oh, God, how strong and hot this
wind is!"?

And why now were her hands trembling, right there on
the window sill? Why did she have to stand and watch the
wind blowing down the street and the darkness swallowing
the edges of the walls, and why . . . ah, look! No, no, it
wasn't a dream, and her eyes were not deceiving her—there

she was on the corner of the street, Smiljka, and he was walking beside her! No, no, it wasn't he; he had been slimmer, he had held himself straighter, and this man beside Smiljka walked awkwardly and did not know what to do with his hands.

But now her eyes were not deceiving her. They were coming toward her. No, they would not stop beneath her window; she knew they would not. No, her eyes were not to blame for what she saw. Oh, God, he was taking her hand; no, he wanted to take leave of her. No! No! It was not by mere chance that they continued on their way.

Once again the street followed them up the hill as it had done the previous day, the day before that, a year ago, and once again she was left alone standing behind the window. . . . No, the window was behind her and somebody had opened the door and a gentle voice was sighing, "Oh, God, how strong and hot this wind is!"—one lone voice, and yet, except for herself, there was nobody in the room.

*   *   *   *

Smiljka leaned back against the rusty fence. Dry twigs crackled. There was an acrid smell of burning in the air, and this smell went straight to the head.

"Well?" he said, taking her hand.

"Don't," she said, drawing gently away.

He leaned against the fence beside her, and the dry twigs crackled again. The wind wrapped the ends of their raincoats around their legs.

"What are you thinking about now?" he asked.

"I'm not thinking about anything," she answered.

"Yes you are."

"Yes . . ."

He shifted away a few paces, and his steps echoed dully in the silence. He wanted to say something more, but the wind began to blow harder, ruffling his hair. He ran his fingers through the tousled locks to smooth them down.

"The wind is so strong and hot," she said.

"I know," he said.

"No, you don't know."

"I do know. The wind was like this when he . . ."

The young man leaned back against the fence, and once again the dry twigs crackled.

"No, no, no, no! You don't know," she cried.

She seemed to him to be choking with tears. "No," he said. "I really don't know." Then he caught her hand again, and once more she drew away gently.

"It's true. You don't know."

"I don't want you to start telling me all over again, because I still won't know." He drew in his breath, as if he were on the point of bursting into tears. He gazed at her, spat out the end of his cigarette and then, without saying a word, strode off, down the road.

"Wait, wait," she called after him. She held her gaze steadily upon him. Now she could feel how much he desired her. When they reached the other end of the street, she offered him her lips. The wind played with their hair, tangling it between their foreheads. She could feel through her coat the pressure of his hands on her hips, and she knew that the wind was strong and hot and that it was playing with their hair.

*   *   *   *

She did not stop crying until the wind rattled the gate after Smiljka.

She began crying again when she went to bed. She wept loudly, inconsolably.

She had not wept like this, she thought, even when they had brought him in the beautifully made coffin. And it seemed to her that she had not wept at all when they carried him to the graveyard. She had walked in front, right behind the coffin, and though she had been sick at heart she had held herself upright. She could hear the music clear-

ly, as though it were sounding in an emptiness, and she
could hear Smiljka at her side crying her heart out with the
unrestrained tears of a young girl. She had walked slowly
along the street, stealing quick glances at the people on the
pavement. She had tried to see if anyone was smiling. But
they were all sunk in thought, and the men had removed
their hats. Some women on the pavement were weeping.
She had been too sick to weep at that time; only her eyelids were raw and heavy. But she could hear the women on
the pavement weeping and was grateful to them. Then the
music had stopped and started up again. Smiljka had cried
all the time.

Oh, God, she had not cried so much when her son died.
Why was she crying so much now? Was it because she felt
as if she were dead and because there would be nobody to
weep for her above her grave?

*   *   *   *

He is gone, he is gone, she thought, as she leaned against
the gate, the wind tugging at the ends of her coat, blowing
through her open blouse and straying over her body. Why
does this wind not stop?

Later, when she lay in her bed beneath the window, gazing at the patch of sky fretted with the dry branches of the
tree, she began to sink back into the past—who knows how
many times she had already done so—back to that point
where something had to be brought to light, to be understood.

She was sixteen years old then. It was early spring. That
spring raced through her like a warm sea breeze, the clanging
of the school bell rang out loud through the strident shriek
of the sirens and the noise of the airplanes, and a flower
pressed between her hands died and fell into the dust of
the road leading toward the air-raid shelter.

One day the town siren did not sound, the airplanes did
not come roaring through the gentle blue air, and the small

flower did not die in the dust of the road leading toward the shelter. That day the blue twilight, melted by a stream of yellow sunlight, came to rest in the young schoolgirl's eyes, and the gray houses, the twisting streets, and the budding trees all contracted into these eyes. And at home these eyes shone mistily between four walls and were dappled with the many colors of bright desire.

He was waiting in front of the gate, his coat unbuttoned, his hands thrust deep into his trouser pockets. They made their way in silence toward the garden where the railway tracks ran through the young meadows along the embankment. He held her close to him among the flowering trees, and she, as always, rested her head on his shoulder and began to sink into a pleasant fear.

Later, they sat down on the grass and had watched the rays of the late afternoon sun glancing off the railway tracks. The fields grew imperceptibly darker, and the wind sprang up, gently at first, bringing the smell of oil and gasoline fumes from the city. The city always breathed oil and gasoline fumes. He, as usual, did not speak. She watched his hair lifting in the wind. She was glad that the wind blew harder and harder, ruffling his hair and, to her great delight, tossing it over his forehead and into his eyes.

"This wind is so strong and hot," she said. The wind played upon the slender blades of the meadow grass. She felt herself drowning in the music of the wind, and her face and breasts were fired with its warmth.

Then he noticed that darkness had fallen, light and transparent. His head was resting on her legs. She was very tired and could not stir. It seemed to her that he was crying.

"The wind's so strong and hot, isn't it?" he said.

She remained silent. It was pleasant to feel the warmth of the wind. She felt that this would never have happened if it had not been for the wind. But she was not angry with the wind; she only tried once again to imagine it playing with long fingers on the meadow grass.

He kept hold of her hand and stared through the trans-

parent dark into the distance where the railway lines con-
verged, without a single ray of light glancing off them. Far
in the distance a mountain jutted out, stiff and angular,
like the body of a shot bird. She wondered why the wind
could not drive the stench of oil and gasoline fumes from
the air the city breathed out.

A flock of ravens flew past.

"It'll rain tomorrow," he said.

She kept silent.

"It'll rain tomorrow, and there'll be plenty of mud," he
said.

She watched the flock of ravens, cawing as they flew past.
"And the airplanes will be firing their machine guns," he
said. "And then the wind will not be strong and hot. It will
break the branches of the trees and chap the skin of our
hands and faces. And in winter . . . oh, God, the rocks will
be buried under the snow, and our eyes will water from
the cold."

She did not understand. She felt only that the wind
would be angry, that it would break the bare branches and
chap the skin of their hands and faces. She heard the ravens
again, cawing loudly; then he whispered softly to her: "Tomorrow it will rain, and there'll be plenty of mud. And the
airplanes will be firing their machine guns." She knew only
that the next day it would rain and that there would be
plenty of mud and that the airplanes would be firing. She
did not want to think of this. She wanted to focus all her
attention upon the firm pressure of his hand and the warm
sighing of the wind through the meadow grass.

They set off for home, walking side by side but not
touching each other. The wind raced after them.

It was quiet that evening, and she thought, idly, that the
following day, maybe even as early as midnight, the rain
would fall, that there would be much mud, and that the
airplanes would start firing their machine guns.

Early in the morning heavy drops of spring rain began
to fall.

The streets filled with mud.

Around midday the airplanes fired on a column of German lorries.

II

"I've come to give you a hand," said Smiljka.

She knew that Smiljka would say this. Did she really have nothing else to say? Five years, and always the same words. But what else could she have said? She too was unable to think of anything else.

They cleaned the house, and Smiljka said, "Why don't you go to church? I'll do the cleaning."

And so she went to church, happy again, and satisfied, and on her way back she wondered how to prevent her from going, how to talk her into staying.

"I'm going now," said Smiljka when she returned from church.

"Stay a little longer—we can have a pleasant chat," she said.

When the halting conversation became unbearable she went into the kitchen for a moment.

"I'm going now," said Smiljka, when she came back.

"No! Why? Stay a while . . . stay for lunch; we'll have a pleasant chat."

Smiljka stayed for lunch. She looked at the girl and thought that she should have told her not to stay to lunch if she didn't feel like it, but then she saw that Smiljka was on the point of saying, "I'm going now."

"Eat, eat, my dear. I've got cakes as well."

"It's really time I went," said Smiljka after the cakes.

"Yes," she answered.

She stood in the doorway looking after her. When Smiljka turned around and nodded to her once again, she wanted to stop her, to tell her that if she didn't enjoy coming, if it was just an ordeal for her, there was no need for her to stay to lunch. But when Smiljka had gone down the corridor as far as the outside door, she called after her, "Come again. I'm so much alone."

"Yes, I'll come again," said Smiljka. Then she left.

Why, why, she cried, I'm so much alone. Oh Lord, I'm so very much alone! Smiljka, my dear, why don't you say —how beautiful the wind is?

III

When she saw them, after their engagement, walking hand in hand, she was not surprised. It simply struck her as strange that she had only now realized that all this had happened five years ago, when that strong hot wind had whirled its laughter down the street.

*　　*　　*　　*

"I'm going now," said Smiljka.

"No—stay," she said. "We could chat a little longer."

Smiljka knew that she should stay. She wanted to stay. And although she knew that nothing was hidden from the old woman, she wanted to explain everything to her herself. She did not, in fact, have anything to explain. She was getting married, and that was all. "I'm engaged," said Smiljka.

"Yes," she said.

Smiljka was on the verge of tears. Was that all she could say, just—yes.

"I'm going now," said Smiljka.

"Yes, it's time you went."

The smell of greenery wafted in from the street. A gentle breeze fluttered the curtains in front of the window. The old woman was standing by the curtains.

"We all love differently," she said.

Smiljka thought it would be senseless to tell her that in her husband she only wanted to find the old woman's son. She too came and stood by the window looking out on the street. Suddenly the wind filled the street. It scudded along in sudden wild gusts. It flicked the curtains into their faces.

"Oh, God, how strong and hot this wind is," said Smiljka and looked at the old woman.

The suggestion of a smile appeared upon her face.

"Yes . . . but there's no point in your continuing to come here. It will be difficult for both of us," she said. They both stared into the wind. Their minds were fixed on the same thought.

There was something consoling in the strength and warmth of the wind. It softened the parting between these two women who would have to go on living with different memories.

OLIVERA NIKOLOVA

Saturday Evening

I wonder if you'll understand me. I was sitting right opposite him and looking at him as though he were an absolute stranger. Those features, that face, those eyes, and that
slightly naughty, very fetching smile—and only a few hours
before all these things had seemed so close to me, so much
my very own. Even more than that, I loved them. I believed
that I loved them and that they occupied a certain place
inside my head, probably that place which is familiar to us
all, which waits to be filled by someone outside us, to be
filled by something of almost dreamlike beauty. This is the
part of ourselves that we can only try to fill with the delu-
sions and the impossible fabrications of our fantasies. And
so it is our most vulnerable spot, and, because it is unprotected and yet eternally nourished by illusions, it is the most
susceptible to pain. Then suddenly a man comes, and one
feels that what he is offering, although it is niggardly, tight-
fisted, and belied by that smile which is meant to be an

Olivera Nikolova. In Macedonia, and especially in Skopje,
where Olivera Nikolova lives, the position of women in society
is a curious one, indeed. At first glance, among the educated
Slav population, it would seem that—as in many Socialist so-
cieties—women experience a high degree of personal and professional autonomy. But beyond this awareness are other
awarenesses. Among the less educated Albanian or Gypsy popu-
lations it is not uncommon to see daughters sold into marriages.
Among Muslims in Skopje most women cover their faces on
the approach of a male stranger. And although few women of
Skopje wear the folk costumes still so prevalent in Macedonian
villages—it is only rarely that one sees anywhere the men in the
traditional costume—many women in Skopje's old town go about
in the voluminous trousers worn in the time of the Turks.
Olivera Nikolova, who was born in 1936, does not write of
such women. But the modern urban woman of whom she does
write is their sister under the skin.

expression of love (but which may be only a screen behind which he hides his lack of feeling), fills that place which is waiting, open and ready.

This thought struck me, and I studied the features of his face. There was a time when I had been quite carried away by his looks. Even this evening before coming here I had noticed how well my husband looked in his new dark blue suit. I even mentioned this to him. He seemed pleased with himself when I told him.

I remembered that when we were on the point of leaving he had given me a cursory glance and clicked his tongue approvingly, just for the sake of good form. In the end he added that I, too, was looking great. It was only later that I remembered all this, and then it filled me with anger. For only then I remembered the way he had preened himself before the mirror, how he had turned to all sides, peered at his reflection, and moved closer to the smooth surface which had reflected his many different poses—half-smiling, frowning, his face superior, serious, contemplative. I had watched him but had said nothing. It had all seemed so normal; he was always like that. He was never afraid of me, of the possibility that I might laugh at him. I knew him too well. He liked to show off, to be noticed, to be the center of attention or, at least, to have his share of the limelight. If it were not for other people's attention, other people's interest, he would have been at an utter loss. But I had never allowed these mannerisms of his to annoy me before. It had never crossed my mind to try to analyze them, much less to pass judgment on them. For Heaven's sake, he was my man, my husband, and I did love him!

We had come to this place. We usually went out on Saturday evenings, and in choosing he always had the final word. I can remember his saying several times: "No, we're not going there. We're going to this place. I may pay more, but at least I won't have to put up with a bunch of drunks." These words had never before struck me as being unusual. Why then did I now give them so much importance? I think it must be because they revealed something to me, because they quite simply illuminated a thought that had previously been buried, a thought that perhaps I did not even want to discover.

This evening had begun in very much the same way. Once again I had tried to avoid feeling that his words had any particular meaning. Perhaps it was something quite trivial that irked me. Maybe it was his parading in front of the mirror. Maybe it was the new suit, which he wore rather stiffly, although not absurdly so. Something, quite simply, disturbed me. But now I have come to see what it was—right now, when everything about him seems strange to me and when I can tell myself, clearly and decisively, that he means nothing to me. Absolutely nothing. I cannot explain this. I am sad. Full of longing—a painless longing. Maybe I am slipping, really, into the insensibility of middle age.

But that isn't the same. This longing is ferreting something out of me, boring into me, and baring something inside. Mine is not a tranquil state. Maybe that is why I am sad, because little by little I am dragging certain things up to the surface, and, when I examine them in the full light, they threaten my assumptions. Now my strongest feeling seems to be that I have been somehow deceived. Irrevocably deceived. That I have been deceived by someone else or, simply, by myself.

The band was playing. A pleasant song. The music was pleasant. I wanted to abandon myself to the sound as I used to do. We danced twice and I tried to let myself go, but I could not. All the time something was bothering me. I did not have the courage to confess aloud to him that something was troubling me, because at the same time I had a feeling of guilt. I didn't know if I was right or if, perhaps, this feeling of distance and unconcern was not simply due to some psychic tension or even to a fever brought on by the heat. Was it no more than this? Did I have the right to torment him with my petty thoughts which, if they were to be heard aloud, would only be laughed to scorn?

You will all be thinking the same thought, won't you: you chose your husband in your own time, of your own free will. Who forced you into it? Nobody. Well, what now do you want? He seemed strange to me. I felt sad because of something in him which troubled me, but, at the same time, I also felt guilty at allowing myself to be irritated by the behavior of my chosen partner for life. These thoughts reduced me to silence, and I became taciturn and unresponsive; only occasionally did I offer some vague, pointless remark (this made me even unhappier). I felt terribly cut off. It was as though I knew nobody. As though I had nothing to share with anybody. The sense of guilt became stronger in me when I noticed that the conversation was flagging and that the others were casting puzzled looks at me with an unspoken question on their lips: Why is she so sad? My low spirits set a limit on everyone's enjoyment, and I could not forgive myself for this.

We sat alone at the table for a while. When we had come in I had been rather excited, although we had attracted no particular attention. The tables were full. I had begun to tremble with a strange longing and had caught hold of his arm. He's my husband, I had thought at that moment. I can surely take his arm when I feel excited. But he was walking in front of me, cutting a path through the tightly packed dancers and following the waiter who was leading us toward a free place at a table in the corner. When he felt my touch he pulled his elbow slightly in to his side, away from my hand. This isn't the time for being tender, he seemed to be saying. He had done this before, and I had always accepted it. But now I had been hurt. Why?

We sat down, and he ordered beer. They brought us two foaming glass mugs with handles. The sides were embossed with half-moons. The waiter was in a great hurry. He left the glasses in front of us on the tray, bowed briskly, and went away. With an elegant, studiously polite gesture my husband placed one glass in front of me and one in front of himself. Despite my qualms I could not help wondering at the way in which he so dutifully but unfeelingly conformed to the accepted forms of politeness.

I watched him and the other two men and the woman who by now had returned to our table. The woman was engaged to one of the men. She seemed highly pleased both with herself and with her good fortune because, as far as I could make out, she was sure she meant a great deal to her fiancé. Clearly, then, she did not feel rejected or abandoned—far from it; she felt that she was a person of importance and that it was up to her to keep their party alive. It was just this self-assurance which seemed to vitalize her. She never stopped chattering. She talked about everything and was quite unabashed by the futility of her jokes; indeed, she seemed to have no time even to register their effect. Her fiancé was touching her, no doubt proud at having such a girl, and smiling before she even finished what she was saying. The young girl, I noticed, often looked at the other man at the table. No doubt she felt she was doing him a favor and that he would enjoy this evening all the more if he could fantasize her interest in him. Or did she want to impress upon him through her show of satisfaction that women such as herself were rare? Is that what she wanted, and had I, too, once been like that?

And my husband? He mattered most because he seemed so like a stranger to me. I amused myself by watching the various shapes into which his lips formed themselves. His voice could be heard above everything, that voice so melodious, so deliberately captivating. He was talking on and on about something, but I wasn't following. I had no interest in what he might be saying; I found him boring. He was interesting only if one observed him without listening to the voice, if one looked just at the features, the body, the movements. He became somehow powerless before the disenchanted eye, crippled without his voice, naked before one's pure observation. He would be uncomfortable if he knew how powerless he was. I cherished this awareness.

He frequently raised his glass and then smacked his lips as though he were tasting the beer for the first time. His face had taken on a ruddy flush, and it pleased me that he could not control this unflattering color. My delight in this small humiliation gave savor to my thoughts. His words came somewhat faster than before; some were irrelevant; he waved his hands, unconscious of the effect he was making. I caught the drift; he was talking about hunting dogs. As he spoke he produced all kinds of nonverbal sounds and irrelevant movements; he whistled as though he were giving signals, and his shining eyes moved from side to side. Then he began to sing quietly with the music. I remembered what he had said about not wanting to be stuck with a bunch of drunks. I could feel a malicious joy rising inside me. No matter how much I hated myself for taking bitter pleasure in his petty weaknesses, I could not forgo such hidden revenge. Up until now he had always been stronger than I, and I had always believed he was right whenever he teased me about anything. Like a cowering dog, I always waited for that mocking laugh of his, but this time I was the stronger. It was my turn to laugh at him. I was going to do my utmost to hold on to this superiority I had gained, although I could feel it was weakened by my woman's powerlessness and pettiness.

Now it was clear to me. At last. From the very beginning of our acquaintance what had disturbed me was his assumption of superiority. I was always in his shadow. He was the important one, he was the one who always spoke, and everybody looked at him. Perhaps I should have been proud to have such a husband. Women like leaders and protectors. But why was I now revolting against him? Somewhere deep within me another thought gnawed at me; I would feel guilty if I allowed this rebelliousness and dissatisfaction to take a grip on me.

Several things that evening had given an edge to this dissatisfaction. He had a new suit; I was wearing an old dress. His antics in front of the mirror had remained in my mind for a long time, although in our haste I had not reflected upon them. He had refused my arm when we came in; he had been so full of himself, dominating the conversation all evening (he wanted to strike an attitude, and he seemed not to care how I regarded him, for he was saying words I had heard many times). His show of gallantry with the beer glasses had irked me, and I found his drunken loquacity forced and silly. Was I simply envious of his new suit? I don't know. What mattered was that all this added bitterness to a dissatisfaction that had been pent up for too long and was now flooding my mind.

I lowered my head so as not to have to look at that familiar face and also, perhaps, to prevent him from noticing my dumb revolt. He means nothing to me—nothing, I repeated. But I still looked up to him; even now he held power over me. When we returned home he would laugh away my childish longings with a superior smile. HE was never in doubt. I was always the one who made the apologies.

But now that I felt him to be only an acquaintance, now that I realized how remote he really was from me, now that I knew he was not my man, why did I not stand up and leave the table? Why did I not put an end to all this with a single movement? Why did I put up with him? If I did so, I thought, it would be the end of everything. This thought thrilled and frightened me. Although I could not bear him, although I knew that from this night on I would not love him, I was more frightened than thrilled. Why? Was it not because of that age-old submissiveness which had been infused into me from my mother's blood?

I sat and sat. I made no attempt to move. I raised my head. I looked at him. He was still remote to me—very, very distant. The young girl was chattering. A long time passed. I had one dance with the man who was not engaged. My husband was drunk. He was talking, swaying contentedly at the table, his legs stretched out; he was looking around.

When I returned to my place, I realized that there was

only one thought in my mind. This Saturday evening must never, never be repeated. I did not try to make any other decisions. An instinctive feeling in me seemed to be stirring up my dissatisfaction to a boiling point. In the end, the guilt I felt was beginning to convince me that I could not remain sad for ever.

VLADA UROŠEVIĆ

The Tailor's Dummy

At midday the writer carried the dummy across the square. It was an ordinary tailor's dummy with a wooden base and no head. The beggars and town loafers abandoned their places in the shade and stared after him for a long time.

The writer had a hard time getting the dummy upstairs. "Who're you carrying that thing for?" asked his neighbor, passing on his way out to the market. "Nobody," the writer panted, dragging the dummy along as one supports an unconscious man, holding it around the waist. The staircase was narrow, and the climbing became more and more difficult; the base of the dummy kept bumping against the bannisters. Finally the writer reached the door of his garret flat. He leaned the dummy against the wall and took the key from under the doormat.

"It's shameful," said Lilla when she came to visit him that afternoon. "Who said you could use my dresses like that?" The writer was standing in the middle of the room, surveying his work with satisfaction. The dummy was dressed in various odds and ends Lilla had left behind in

Vlada Urošević is best known as the leader of a group of poets whose interests lead them away from local and national themes and in the direction of the mainstream of contemporary European poetry. Urošević was born in Skopje in 1934 and attended school and university there. He is now employed as a television editor with Skopje Radio–TV. He is also an editor, a critic, and a translator from Serbo-Croatian.

In addition to his critical and poetic writing, which is known throughout central Europe and has been translated into several languages, Urošević is an accomplished fictionist. His novel, _The Taste of Peaches_ (1965), was widely praised, as were his stories, collected in 1969 under the title, _Signs_.

his flat one day at the end of spring after she brought them back from the dry cleaner's. On the stump of the neck the dummy now had a plaster cast of the head of Aphrodite. Adorning the head was a large, black straw hat.

The writer was highly satisfied with what he had done. The head had been set slightly askew so the hat partly obscured the face, and the dummy looked out from under the brim as though it were trying to win affection. Lilla shrugged, made a grimace of disgust, and turned away. "You might use your time more intelligently," she said. "You haven't written a thing for ages. Instead of writing you just act the fool."

" 'Go and find me if you can,' " the writer began reciting sadly, " 'a word as simple as a stone. . . .' "

Lilla was becoming impatient. "I don't understand you," she said. "I don't understand this joke of yours with the tailor's dummy. I hope you aren't sleeping with it!"

"I need to be constantly surrounded by the characters I'm writing about," he explained. "I must live with my heroes. I'm writing a story, you know, about a man who falls in love with a tailor's dummy."

"Charming," said Lilla. She decided to take away the pieces of clothing that were hanging on the tailor's dummy, but in the end she changed her mind. Outside, the city was choking in orange-colored dust, in the stench from the rubbish bins and the heavy smell from the shrunken river. She crossed to the door and went out onto the balcony. Down below, in the back yard, on the stark white concrete, some half-naked boys were sitting and cracking apricot pips. The other part of town, across the river, was the yellowish color of faded postcards.

A tiny figure was walking along the street waving its arms and looking up. "Here comes the painter," said Lilla. "We can't hide from him; he's seen me. Now he'll stay till midnight."

The painter was delighted with the dummy. "It's superb!" he shouted, gesticulating extravagantly. "It reminds me of my student days. When I was at the Academy we never had any money for models, so we had to paint tailor's dummies. There are some dummies!"

The painter stayed a long time. The stars were hardly visible in the summer sky; they were smothered by the exhalations of the city, the moisture hanging in the air, the smoke. "That's the constellation of Sagittarius," mumbled the painter, pointing vaguely somewhere above the tops of the skyscrapers.

Then the three of them went out together. The painter was in raptures over the dummy and promised to paint it. He was sweating. The city was trapped beneath the stifling heat, and the baked air that had been sealed into the walls all day was only now escaping through the bricks. The people walked with difficulty along the streets; there was a sickly gleam in their eyes, and they were jumpy and irritable.

The following day, when Lilla went to visit the writer, she met his landlady on the staircase. "I've had just about as much as I can take of all this!" shouted the landlady, flushed and panting. "As much as I can take. First it's a girl, and now it's some kind of ghost and a tailor's dummy!" The landlady turned around as Lilla squeezed past her. "Find somebody else!" she shouted. "That man of yours is undressing a freak up there, an antique freak!"

"What's going on?" asked Lilla as she walked into the room.

The writer smiled bitterly. "It's all so stupid," he said. "First thing this morning, in came the man to collect for the electricity. I was on the balcony. Suddenly he screamed and ran down the stairs. A little later the landlady suddenly appeared. I was just setting up the dummy when she came in." The dummy was wearing a theatrical wig. The long red hair tumbled down in waves over its shoulders.

"How's the story getting on?" asked Lilla.

"I'm still mulling it over," said the writer. "It'll be an excellent story. D'you feel like going out?"

As they were saying goodbye, the writer asked Lilla for her sunglasses.

The following day Lilla found the dummy wearing her sunglasses. The dark glasses made a strong contrast with the white plaster head; it seemed as though from behind them the dummy was keeping an eye on everything that happened in the room. "You're crazy," said Lilla. "I won't allow you to use my sunglasses like this."

The writer tried to calm her. "That's you," he said, pointing to the dummy. "When I'm writing about the dummy, I think about you. It's your twin."

"Don't you mix me up in all this," said Lilla. "I don't want to be replaced by anybody—no matter who. I hope you don't take it to bed with you!"

"Don't be such a little goose," smiled the writer. "It's only a dummy."

"You're beginning to frighten me," said Lilla. "I don't understand you any more."

" 'Go and find me if you can,' " the writer began reciting, " 'a word as simple as a stone . . .' "

"All the same," said Lilla, "I don't like this game of yours with the dummy."

"The story'll soon be ready," said the writer soothingly. "It'll be a splendid story. A young man who falls in love with a tailor's dummy. You'll see what a sensation it will be."

"Are we going out tonight?" asked Lilla. "There's a good Greek film showing at the open-air cinema."

"All right," said the writer. "I just have a little more to add." He stuck some cheap, shiny buckles into the dummy's hair, stepped back a few paces, and surveyed it with satisfaction. Then he jotted down something in his notebook. "It gets more and more beautiful, don't you think?" he asked. Lilla was silent. She made a point of facing the other way.

In front of the open-air cinema they met the painter. He was eating peanuts. "How's the story getting on?" he asked at once.

"Splendidly," said the writer. "I've worked out a new ending. It'll be a kind of absolute story."

"Let's hurry," said Lilla. "It looks as if the tickets are nearly all sold."

The writer said he was going to work for the following few days. Lilla did not come to visit him. Only when she finally got bored of going to the cinema alone did she climb up to his garret flat one evening. The dummy was standing in the middle of the room. The writer was lying on his bed. The light was not switched on.

"It's terribly stuffy in here," said Lilla. "You never air the place. Have you been out at all?"

"I've been busy writing," he answered. "The story's almost finished."

Lilla made a wide detour around the dummy, stopped by the bed, and sat down. "Now that the story's almost finished, will you clear that dummy out of here?" One could detect in her a voice a scarcely concealed note of hatred toward that wooden figure dressed in her clothes.

"Don't be impatient," said the writer. "The dummy should be allowed to stay for a while. The young man in the story is very much in love with it." The half darkness that filled the room was thick and sticky. There was a smell of unwashed clothes, of sweat. The fetid air hung in the limp rags.

"Are we going to go anywhere?" asked Lilla.

"Not this evening," said the writer.

"Tomorrow?" asked Lilla.

"Yes, tomorrow," said the writer with a sigh. "I still have something left to write this evening."

"All right," said Lilla, rising. "Wait for me tomorrow in the café on the quay."

The first person Lilla met the next day was the painter. He told her he had seen the writer in the café on the quay. "What happened to the dummy?" the painter shouted after her when they had already said goodbye.

"Nothing," said Lilla. "But something's going to happen soon."

She climbed up the staircase, afraid that the landlady might spot her. She found the key under the doormat and opened the door. The dummy was standing in the middle of the room. Lilla walked up to it, slowly and cautiously, as though she were approaching a living being. She was overwhelmed with a sense of disgust and tore the wig from the plaster head. The bald plaster crown shimmered in the moonlight.

She quickly undressed the dummy. The brooches and buckles tumbled to the floor, where they cracked and shattered under her feet. Her hands trembled as she burnt the wig and the pieces of clothing in a small stove full of old papers. The room smelt of smoke.

She took the plaster head, opened the balcony door and leaned over the rail. The white blob of the head described a neat arc in the twilight; then there was a light explosion as the plaster shattered on the concrete paving of the yard. The cats fled from the rubbish bins, meowing with fright.

Lilla then threw the dummy itself from the balcony. The wood clattered loudly on the ground. A light was turned on outside, somewhere in the yard. An elderly voice could be heard shouting: "Have you gone mad? I'm going to call the police!" Lilla quickly left the room, closed the door, and ran downstairs.

Excited voices could be heard in the yard. Doors were being opened. She thought she glimpsed several people gathering. She ran out into the street and kept running until she reached the corner. Then she walked slowly.

She had already recovered her calm by the time she came to the quay. She had seen the writer from a distance; he was sitting in front of the café, drinking beer.

"Hot, isn't it?" she said as she sat down.

"Terrible," said the writer. "D'you want a beer?"

"If it's cold," said Lilla. "I'm terribly thirsty."

"I've finished the story, you know," said the writer. "It's ready at last. I wrote the end yesterday. D'you know how it finishes?"

Lilla drank her beer and simply raised her eyebrows curiously.

"The girl who loves him," said the writer, "goes to his place when he isn't there and destroys the dummy."

Lilla lowered her unfinished glass.

"It's a strange story," the writer went on. "A kind of absolute story. This young man who falls in love with the dummy is writing a story. The story is about how a young man, who is in love with a dummy, writes a story. And he writes the story." The expression on Lilla's face was cold. Under the neon light her face had a lifeless sheen as though it were made of plaster.

"Hurry up," said the writer. "Drink your beer. I want to go back to my place and read you the story."

Lilla managed to speak only when they reached the staircase. "What happens at the end of the story?" she asked.

"Oh," said the writer as he unlocked the door, "when the writer sees that she's destroyed his dummy, he strangles the girl. Funny, isn't it?"

VLADIMIR KOSTOV

The Game

It was exactly two o'clock in the afternoon when L.M. arrived at his apartment on the top floor of an apartment block. The room he entered was very sparsely furnished. It was quite empty but for a bed, a table, and a chair. There was no carpet on the floor. For the next ten minutes L.M. was free to play with a noose at the end of a rope. He picked it up and began trying to lasso the door handle. Out of thirty throws—one for each year of his age—he caught the handle seven times: a record.

He smiled to himself. But with him a smile was not an expression of delight. He seemed to be mocking something within himself. He became lost in his thoughts. Gradually his face took on a terrible expression, an ugly look. This was the ugly look of an exceptionally handsome man, well-built, with even features.

L.M. seemed like a man resolved to do anything, come what may. He remained for a while in his tense position

Vladimir Kostov. Although Macedonian fiction is still created to a large extent within the traditions of realism, a number of writers are engaged in antirealistic experiments. Vladimir Kostov is one. Not only does his work show significantly the influence of such writers as Joyce and Beckett, but in his recent collection, *The Game* (1969)—the story here is the title story from the collection—Kostov has shown a willingness to experiment radically in what has come in the West to be known as the antistory.

Kostov was born in Bitola in 1932 and completed his schooling there. Afterwards he studied at Skopje, taking his degree in Yugoslav literature there and then returning to Bitola, where he is presently a member of the faculty at the Teachers' Training College. He has written two novels, *Faces with Masks* (1967) and the celebrated and honored *Mara's Wedding* (1968). A third novel, *A New Mind*, and another collection of short stories appeared in 1970.

and then passed his hand over his face. His expression now changed, becoming gentle and slightly weary. He looked at the clock: ten past two. He crossed to the window, opened it wide, and stood beside it, holding the noose.

A yellow bumblebee droned noisily past him. L.M. tried to follow its flight but then lost sight of it. Then he suddenly glimpsed it again, darting like an arrow toward the small park. Children there were playing a game of some sort. One of them noticed the bumblebee and scampered after it. The others joined in the chase. Some of them stripped off their shirts and flapped them at the bumblebee. It seemed they had hit the insect and stunned it. Now began the shouting. Now began the relentless chase.

It was no longer a game for the bumblebee, but a desperate battle for life. He must, in some way, have been aware of the fate awaiting him at the children's hands, for just as the children were on the point of catching him, he always managed, at the last moment, to give them the slip.

The children felt as though they had lost an important battle. A young mother appeared on one of the lower balconies of the building across the way. She called to her children. It seemed she had just returned from somewhere, probably from work. She was tying on her apron as she came out onto the balcony. She was wearing a low-cut, sleeveless blouse. No doubt she had just put it on and had been in too great a hurry to button it all the way up, for a large expanse of snow-white, smooth, plump breast could be seen. Two children broke away from the group. One child was about six years old, the other about three. Both were fair, smooth, and plump, and they resembled their mother in other ways as well.

L.M. looked again at the clock: a quarter past two. He ran his eye along the concrete path near the apartment block opposite him. Just as his gaze reached the end of the concrete path, a cheerful young girl appeared round the corner of the building.

She was, to all appearances, an officeworker coming

home from her job. Clearly she was one of those girls, cheerful by nature, who sing their way through life. People usually say they are mischievous. But it is not cunning that makes them mischievous. It all stems from their lively fancy, which conjures up innumerable ways of expressing their joy in life. Because of their cheerful nature they may seem, at first sight, to be too much open to persuasion. But this is not the case. They are ambitious, sensitive, and full of character. They are ready for great love and great sacrifices. In love they offer everything and demand everything. Happiness and unhappiness are only one step apart for them. And they often take this step. They are often left in the lurch, abandoned and insulted. This is a terrible shame.

As she came round the side of the building, she glanced briefly up at L.M.'s window and, when she had spotted him, quickly dropped her eyes. She was overcome with delight. She could not conceal her smile. It delighted and amused her that he was holding the noose in his hand. She wanted to take a firm grip on herself and avoid looking a second time in L.M.'s direction, but some force stronger than herself compelled her to do so, and once again she looked up toward his window. L.M. seized her gaze and held it captive for a time.

As they stared at each other they exchanged loving smiles. She was angry at herself and reproachful of her own weakness in not being able to resist the temptation to look up. But her reproaches were not seriously meant, for they vanished as soon as she reached the middle of the path opposite his window. Once again she looked up, expecting him to wave the noose at her, as he had usually done for the past few days.

He did indeed wave it in her direction. This was his way of saying, symbolically, that he intended to catch her, to draw her close to his breast and make her his own, there, in his flat. Pretending to be angry both with him and herself, to oppose his plan, and to refuse their mischievous game, she ran along the path hoping to "escape," to "save" herself. But when she reached the door she was to enter, she glanced up furtively once again at L.M. and thus betrayed the fact that she wanted to be caught, to be drawn close to his breast, and to be taken there in his flat.

She walked through the door, but he did not altogether lose sight of her. For a certain time, for two whole minutes, he followed her silhouette through the frosted glass wall beside the staircase, almost until the moment when she was to reemerge on her balcony—from where, according to the rules of the game, she was to cast him the last glance.

She appeared on the balcony and looked at him. It now was a look full of warning, a look begging him to play the game fairly and reminding him that love should not be played with or the game might end tragically. L.M. called up all his powers of expression, assuring her with one look that he would play fair and that he wished her the greatest happiness on earth. She believed him. She was thankful to him. She smiled at him most tenderly. She wanted to withdraw, but she was not able. She was not able to tear her eyes away from his face.

His was the face of a fine-looking man with expressive, noble, and strangely tender features. At such times L.M. was irresistibly handsome. The girl could have stood and stared at him like this for much, much longer. But she dared not allow herself such a pleasure. She called up all her strength and withdrew.

L.M. was unable for a long time to take his eyes off the balcony, off the spot where she had stood. Then, suddenly, a change came over his face; some gloomy thought passed over it like a dark shadow. L.M. drew his hand across his face.

He turned back toward the inside of his room. Great sorrow overwhelmed him. He shook his head wretchedly and pressed his hand to his brow. He tried to get a grip on himself, but he could not. He let out a desperate cry, "Ah!" Something dreadful was tormenting him. His face contorted, and his limbs jerked. He beat his temples with his fists, then burst into tears. In desperation he covered his face with his hands and collapsed onto the bed.

Then he felt easier and only cried. He cried for a long time. He could not control his tears. After an hour he quieted and fell asleep.

I

The same day. Almost seven o'clock in the evening. L.M. left behind him the district of concrete apartment blocks and went into the old part of town. Here the walls were dry and cracked by the summer heat.

It seemed to L.M. that the moon was also dry, a splinter in the sky. It seemed to him almost motionless; it seemed to creak as it moved. At any moment it might fall into one of the streets and shatter into a thousand fragments.

Entering one of the buildings, he asked if this was where the teacher lived who had advertised French lessons in the newspaper. It was. The teacher was about thirty-five years old, pale and ugly. She had a solid, heavy, awkward body, but her voice was soft and gentle.

L.M. introduced himself as an archivist from the Oriental section of the Historical Archives. He needed to learn French because, if he could become proficient in the language, he might be sent for several months to work in the Paris archives and libraries. Although his voice was calm, he seemed tired. She invited him in.

He entered a long, dark corridor. She let him go ahead of her, but he waited for her to lead the way, not so much out of politeness as from the desire to get a good look at her backside. He slowed down his pace, staring at the heavy outlines of her thighs. However, he soon realized that she was ashamed of this particular feature of her body, and when she sensed that he was staring at her, she smiled shyly and pressed herself against the wall, hiding her backside and letting him walk on ahead. He changed places with her, endeavoring through his naive expression to assure her that there had been in his thoughts no hint of erotic desire nor any intention whatsoever of secretly indulging in the sensuality of her fleshiness.

Somewhat later he broke the silence. A scientific dispute was being waged concerning an agreement between the Sultan Sheytan Ali Suleiman and one of the French kings. "I have twice published papers in *Historical Survey*," he explained, "and in them I have presented points of view which have conflicted with those of the renowned Professor Banda. The opportunity of working in one of the French archives would certainly assist me in establishing my theory and in the solution of one of the crucial problems in the sphere of Oriental studies. As far as the Institute is concerned, they are willing to aid me by financing my stay in Paris. The Director is particularly well disposed towards this plan, for he sees it as an excellent opportunity for me to establish my reputation."

She stared at him in astonishment. L.M. realized that he had to a considerable extent abandoned that modesty which, according to the game, should have been the basis for all later success, and so he hastened to repair the impression he had made on her. He implied that he was a man to be admired for his well-balanced attitude to life as well as a person who could justly assess his own capacities.

He said, "The Director of the Institute is unjust to set my abilities at such a low rate, but the Head of the Archives is even more unjust for setting them at a still lower rate. Looking at things realistically, I have already achieved something, thanks to my honest work and to the love I cherish for historical research. But this bothers the boss. The fact that I place the interests of scholarship above career disturbs him greatly.

"Bureaucrats are harmful people, Katerina, and the most harmful among them are those who hold posts in scientific institutes. They put a brake on progress. They represent the striking force of reactionary opinion in the world. They are allied to those powers which ruthlessly plunge the world

into wars and which have brought the world today face to
face with ultimate destruction. My boss does not see that
it is people like himself who are responsible for the world
situation. And perhaps people feel that a man who studies
the times which have passed cannot be held accountable for
the problems of his own times.

"Permit me to observe that this man is carrying out his
work for the sake of his own worldly interests. It is enough
to say that he has pawned his conscience to buy his wife
a fur coat and sold her, together with the fur coat, so as to
worm himself into the position he now holds. I could prove
his guilt as irrefutably as I can prove that one and one are
two. But this is forbidden.

"It is most strictly forbidden to prove that one and one
are two. You may prove anything you like—the laws gov-
erning outer space, the formulae shaping nuclear science,
electronics, or higher mathematics—but it is most strictly
forbidden to prove that one and one are two.

"Do you remember Giordano Bruno? Naturally he was
made to suffer. Or Galileo Galilei? They proved, first and
foremost, the simple truth that one and one are two. The
Church was frightened of this. This was something the
Church could not forgive. This was an unpardonable heresy.
This was the source of all evil, all conflicts, all wars, all
catastrophes. And from this heresy stems the possibility of
a nuclear war."

L.M. noticed that Katerina had been keeping her eyes
fixed on him. He was also aware that they were sitting directly opposite each other at the table. Suddenly the image
of her round knees under the table came into his mind. It
occurred to him that he might touch her knees with his own,
but he restrained himself at the last moment.

He immediately set about correcting the tactical errors
in his game and restoring the rhythm. He listened to what
Katerina was saying and was somewhat surprised to find
that she had divined the allegory behind his tirade, but she
seemed to be hypersensitive and had apparently grasped

the fact that he was alluding to her interest in material gain
or, rather, to her desire to make a little money on the side
by giving private lessons.

In justification of this interest she told him of the deep
love she felt toward books and fine literature and explained
that her regular salary was too modest to allow her the
luxury of buying such books. For this reason she had created
a special fund made up from the proceeds of her private
lessons. All this was most discreetly explained in order to
dispel any unfavorable impression she might have left on
L.M.

He now felt ready to give his virtuoso performance. The
situation had now reached the stage at which flattery could
be used to the greatest advantage, for by praising her he
could improve his own esteem in her eyes and also could
hint at the possibility of an intimate relationship between
them. He began by expressing his approval of her explanation and his deep respect for her passionate interest in
culture. At the same time he most tactfully drew her attention to the affinity between their spiritual interests and
thus, by inference, to the probable affinity between their
characters.

She appeared to be highly satisfied by his suggestion.
Listening to him was a pleasure. "No, no," he said, "I'm not
flattering you. It's absolutely true, believe me. Evolution
and revolution have their beginnings in rooms filled with
bookshelves and desks. You are the beginning of evolution
and I—of revolution. It is only a short step from one to the
other."

A charming smile played over Katerina's lips. "Have you
read Hyde?" he asked. "Yes? No? His *Lover's Lament*?"
He explained to her who Hyde was and assigned him a very
high place in the history of literature, for he wanted to
demonstrate his superior knowledge in the field of literature as well.

Katerina, with typical feminine acquiescence, conceded
to his superiority. He promised next time to bring her his

own rare copy of *Lover's Lament*, which, unfortunately, was not only coverless but also missing the first two pages. This, however, would not prevent her from gaining an acquaintance with the great writer and seeing for herself how he had been the victim of ill fortune and had thus been prevented from becoming as famous as certain other less talented writers of his time. "Hyde," he said, "will be resurrected; his day will also come, and the impartiality of time will triumph. I stand for the triumph of justice. Injustice pains me, no matter whether it comes from the Director of the Historical Archives or from the false judgment of literary criticism, which is fashioned and refashioned by numerous men in positions of authority."

His voice was charged with just the right amount of anger. Fire shone in his eyes. A lump of fury stuck in his throat, and in his effort to clear it, he went through all the customary grimaces. This was all in conformity with the rules of the game. His plan was developing perfectly.

He became silent. He was giving her time to work up a passionate love for Hyde and for justice and so, through them, to begin desiring him as well. He was forced, because of her hypersensitivity, to make certain changes in his plan in order to speed the event. The ease with which she had permitted him to capture all the key positions in her defense was far beyond his expectations. So too was the ease with which she had allowed him to set traps where she least expected them.

L.M. stood up to leave. She followed him to the outer door. They shook hands. He kept hold of her hand for a long time. Then he told her something which no rule in the game prevented him from saying. In this situation his honesty came to him quite without warning; it seized him fiercely; it swept away all that had been built up through the game.

He said, "Of one thing I am sure. The moon will drop tonight. I fear it may land on my head. If it falls, then it will fall as the shells did in the First World War. My father told me about that, about how the shells fell in the First World War. First you heard the sound they made, then you saw them flying through the air. People regulated their lives according to the flight of the shells. But there were some who were unable to escape. They were left standing bolt upright like statues in the street. The shells fell on their heads."

The only way Katerina could react to what he had said was to try to pass it off as a joke. This gave rise to a most ridiculous state of affairs. He averted his face to avoid having to look at her. "Ah!" he cried, in despair.

II

Katerina was sunk in an armchair. *Lover's Lament* was lying open on her lap. A smile played about her lips. She pretended to herself that she was delighted at having such a wonderful work in her hands, but her delight was not for the book. She was unconsciously feeling an affection toward L.M. and a satisfaction at having him close to her, this man whose intimate personal and spiritual secrets she knew.

L.M. was absolutely sure of the power he held over her, and so he decided to faint this very evening. This was a favorite ruse of his, a procedure tried and tested in every situation. He wanted to avoid making the mistake that had spoiled his affair with the lawyer's wife, and so he determined to remain strictly within the limits of the game and to make sure that he did not ruin everything at the end by falling into a fit of despair and admitting to his hoax.

Even if one of his fits overcame him (as was not impossible, if one considered the shattered state of his nerves recently), and even if he did not succeed in concentrating all his power upon the need to serve his baser motives, he would, at least, never admit to the hoax. He would not admit to it at any cost. He was quite crafty enough to dupe this naive and inexperienced woman.

Katerina was wearing a new dress, which was cut slightly short, in timid deference to the new fashion for tight, skimpy dresses. She felt at ease in the armchair, mostly because it helped to conceal the all-too-evident plumpness of her figure. This sense of security even lent her a hint of coquettishness. She pretended to be looking at the book, but all the time she was conscious that L.M. was making an effort to catch her eye, so as to express more openly the spiritual ties that united them. She did not wish to oppose his desire, but she was shy.

Finally she summoned her courage and looked up at him. Her look was bashful, the look of a guilty person. She soon lost her courage and tried to find a way of concealing the real reason for her glance. She mentioned something in connection with *Lover's Lament*, but her words lacked coherence.

L.M. once again tested the firmness of his desire. He found it firm indeed. He leaned over to the left, closed his eyes, and fell gently to the floor. Katerina screamed, dropped the book, and jumped up to help him.

His head lolled back to the left, his right arm reposed above his heart, his lips remained slightly parted. His breathing was scarcely perceptible. He had in the back of his mind a particular Renaissance painting of a lamentation over Christ. He did his best to imitate Christ's martyred expression.

Katerina was distressed. She was disturbed. She had no idea what to do. She touched his face with her fingers. He slowly opened his eyes.

She quickly withdrew her hand, as though caught in some forbidden act. He gave her a weary smile but did not change his position. He was giving her time to rejoice at his recovery. There was no strength left in his voice; it was practically a whisper.

"Forgive me," he said. "This is the consequence of great spiritual strain. Commitment exhausts the human body but strengthens the soul—to mankind's great good fortune. I'm thirsty."

In the twinkling of an eye she had transformed herself into a compassionate nurse. She demonstrated great tenderness in persuading him to drink. Then she helped him to stand up. He was constantly offering looks of gratitude. "Maybe it would be better if I went," he suggested.

She opposed this suggestion. "No." A note of determination crept into his voice, "Maybe it would be better for me to go and never to return."

"No, no," she objected firmly.

He was persistent: "If I do, I may save both you and myself."

She looked straight into his eyes. She was searching for an explanation. "I came," he said, "intending to confess to you but also to conceal something from you. But it's impossible, Katerina. I've had enough of lying. The time has come for me to account for everything. If I continue with my lies, they could well kill me."

L.M. realized just in time that he was slipping out of step with the rhythm of the game and made an effort to recover himself. Katerina did not dare to utter a word. She was waiting for something momentous to happen. Something momentous in her life.

He stopped staring at the wall and shifted his gaze slowly toward her until his eyes came to rest on her hands, folded in her lap. His voice was full of suffering. "I am alone," he told her. "Utterly alone. Abandoned."

Katerina looked at him pityingly. Her hand strayed out instinctively in search of his. She wanted to touch him. She wanted to let him know that he was not alone, that she was with him. But she realized that this could not be done and so drew back her hand.

L.M. noticed her movement. "Much may be achieved in one person's lifetime," he told her. "There is much, Katerina, which I might have achieved, and maybe there is still much

more waiting for me to achieve. I might, perhaps, have become a general. Or I might have discovered many truths
and unmasked many forms of injustice. But I am alone.
Loneliness is a disease which is gnawing away at my vital
strength. I need care. I need a sympathetic nurse. I need a
kindly hand to point me the way. Otherwise my strength
will vanish, never to return, and my existence will become
senseless."

He was silent for a few moments, sunk in thought and
still staring at her hands lying in her lap. Then he stole a
glance at her face. He seemed to be searching for the courage
to tell her something.

Once again he lowered his eyes, and, as if dissatisfied with
himself for having to say something that should not be
said, he explained, "There are many women. There are
many of them, and they offer themselves for next to nothing. You can come across them at every step. They're a real
danger. They're becoming a danger to decent citizens. I've
known a number of them, but not a single one was able to
offer the love which cures loneliness."

He now looked up and stared, boldly and decisively,
straight into her eyes which, from lack of courage, she lowered. "The only great love," he told her passionately, "is
love at first sight. That is the true, fatal love worthy of im-
mortality. All other forms of love open the way to the vile
demands of the ego."

He broke off for a moment, then continued, "I feel isolated and insignificant in this whirlpool of a world. The sun
is lost in soot and dust. It is blackened with charcoal. I am
lost. I am wandering alone. I need a companion. I need a
faithful companion to travel through life with me. Those
are my words, Katerina. Those are my words. They come
straight from the heart and have never been uttered before;
they have never been profaned. It is not the ego which
drives me to speak to you. I speak to you in the name of
the man within me whom I wish to save. It is up to you

whether you choose to save him or not. I entrust him to the beautiful and noble person I have found you to be."

Then there was silence. She did not dare to utter a word. She did not dare look at him. He thought it would be appropriate to add a few more words: "Maybe I was carried away. It is not impossible. As much as our feelings are worthy of respect, so too are our thoughts. The only truth which is dear to me is that which the mind discovers and the heart confirms. You are the embodiment of that truth. There can be no doubt of it. You are incapable of lying. You are incapable of sinning. I leave it to you to pass judgment, to know what is just and only what is just."

She still did not dare to speak. She still did not dare to make even the slightest movement. "I'm thirsty," he said. "I'm very thirsty." Trembling with awe and respect, she fetched a glass of water.

When she returned and stood trembling before him, L.M. caught her hand. Her plump body began to tremble. The glass slipped out of her hand and broke. He drew her to his breast and placed a gentle kiss on her pale, faded cheeks. She mumbled something unintelligible, as though she were praying.

"I know you want to be alone. I will respect your wish," he said. She looked at him with gratitude. They walked toward the door in silence. He went ahead; she followed. They passed down the long, dark corridor. He stopped; she also stopped.

She was expecting him to say something. "Is your mother still alive?" he asked.

"No." Her voice trembled.

"Nor is mine," he told her. Then he asked another question: "How did you lose your mother?"

She did not answer. He continued: "The Fascists did terrible things to my mother in front of my very eyes. Then they shot her. My father was a patriot. He died in the mountains." They were both silent for a while.

It was dark in the corridor. It was menacingly silent in the corridor. "I'm a bastard child," said Katerina. "I grew up in an orphanage."

"Ah," said L.M. "Ah." He sighed and felt for her hand in the dark. Her hand seemed large and rough. He opened the outer door and was about to walk out when he started back in alarm.

The moon hung naked and lonely in the vault of the sky. "The heavy silver rays are beating down upon my brow. Stay where you are! You must have iron nerves to withstand the moon's fierce strength. And you are fragile. You come from the land of make-believe. You must not at any price expose your chasteness to the rude leer of this lecher of the skies. He will deceive you. He will lead you the wrong way. He may fall at any moment and strike you right in the heart. And you will be unable to escape. You are one of those who do not know how to hide. You are a sacrificial lamb at the altar of the cruel God."

Katerina approved of his words, for, although she had understood nothing, she was convinced he had spoken passionately to her of love. She persisted in offering her cheek to be kissed. The kiss he had given her a short while ago had pleased her. But L.M. did not kiss her. He averted his face to avoid looking at her. "Ah, ah!" he cried, passionately.

III

They climbed up the dazzling white marble stairs. She was wearing a white dress and L.M. a yellow cotton jacket. The guests were already seated at the tables. They were all formally dressed—the women in low-cut dresses and the men in black bow ties. The headmaster of the school was an elegant little man, and bald. He was compactly built and had a fresh, ruddy face. L.M. began to develop the rough outlines of a plan to call on the headmaster in his study one day when classes were being held and then, at some time during their intimate conversation, suddenly to bring down the school stamp hard upon his shiny forehead.

As soon as they had all taken their places the headmaster began his speech. He welcomed the guests and his colleagues and then went on to speak of the school patrons. He concluded with a recital of the school's successes during the past few years, successes he linked to achievements in the rebuilding of the nation.

His speech was as brief as such an occasion demanded, and his delivery was terse, but, at the same time, his excellent diction and his clear articulation were shown off to the best advantage in his masterly turns of phrase. The applause was long and warm. When it began to slacken, L.M. continued clapping alone; thus he encouraged the others to renew their applause.

This brought the headmaster again to his feet. He smiled, showing two rows of neat, white teeth, and made a slight bow. A wave of exaltation swept over L.M. He had been deeply impressed. He felt as though he were trembling all over, as though his spirit were something real and individual. He was overwhelmed by an urge to speak. He could have shouted for joy. Some of the weight of his heavy inner burden found release in the excitement of the situation.

He felt many women's glances resting upon him. He knew that the glances some of the women were sending him were only in their thoughts. He was acutely aware of his power over the sex. His breathing was labored and irregular. His nostrils widened. His mind began to race. He thought of innumerable possible combinations.

But L.M. was in no hurry, so he waited for the first wave of delight to pass. He knew that if he were to surrender himself to it he would experience strong but short-lived satisfaction. L.M. drew on his rich past experience. He did not want to hurry and run the risk of being hasty and flustered at the crucial moment. He did not intend to be misled by any false intensifications or seeming culminations. He wanted to make his approach gradually, to use psychological insight to illuminate the road leading toward his goal, and to snatch up on the way everything that could be seized.

He stood up and raised his glass in a greeting to the guests. He began speaking in a quiet, authoritative voice about a species of night butterfly of the genus *rheopsus* whose very existence represented a positive threat to mankind, for the dust disseminated by its wings, when inhaled, caused certain parts of the human psyche to develop such powerful militaristic tendencies that a third, disastrous, suicidal war would most surely break out.

He observed the interest with which his discussion was followed. This filled him with deep inner delight, and he smiled to himself, but he did not allow his satisfaction to become evident in his voice or manner or to disturb his composure.

In order to dispel any suspicion that his assertion was unfounded, he made specific mention of *Key*, a scientific journal, and also slipped in the names of two eminent biologists—Klaus and Bogomilov. He even turned to the school biology teacher for confirmation of his facts. The biology teacher was in absolute agreement with his explanation and did his best to give the impression that the names and theories L.M. had mentioned were by no means unknown to him.

L.M. thanked him and continued: "We owe a debt of gratitude to science for identifying the inherent cause of the instinct for self-annihilation in night butterflies and for once again offering man, as many times before in our near and distant past, the possibility of combating the cruelty of nature. For nature wages a constant war of aggression upon man's triumphant development and is bent on bringing about his extinction just as surely as it was bent on the annihilation of the mammoth and the dinosaur."

He paused for a moment and cast a stern glance at the faces gazing up at him. A softer note now crept into his voice. "Permit me," he continued, "as the representative of the International Association of *Homo Sapiens* to express my firm conviction that your school will also join us in the campaign for the extermination of night butterflies. The opening ceremonies for the campaign will be held in Geneva, beginning at midnight, Central European Time, on the 26th of August—the day upon which these dreaded insects begin their annual season of propagation."

He gave a brisk nod to show that he had concluded his speech. The audience applauded. The young geography mistress, who was sitting to his left, clapped most enthusiastically. The headmaster did not applaud but glanced inquiringly toward L.M. L.M. sat down and pressed his leg firmly against the young geography teacher's.

She stopped clapping and discreetly withdrew her leg, uncertain of L.M.'s intentions. She had decided to bide her time.

L.M. knew that there was no need for him to wage a tactical war to overcome her pride, since he was sure she did not have any. At first glance his experience had told him that she was given to sensual thoughts and fantasies. Realizing this, he maintained a firm and unmistakable pressure on her leg; thus he forced her to admit her weakness and abandon herself to the rich delights he was offering her.

He brought his head closer to hers and asked with great interest whether the number seven or eight conformed to the geological composition of glaciers in the formula $Czo4 -7$ or -8. At the same time he expressed his doubts concerning the formula's accuracy. She readily indicated that she shared his doubts. He then told her that the $Czo4$ was a mere figment of the imagination, as were Klaus and Bogomilov, whom she had applauded so delightedly.

"You're terribly stupid," he told her. "You're very limited, very unintelligent. Your soul is impoverished. You're an infant, a charming infant. One could play with you like a ball. Throw you and catch you.

"But one would be sadly mistaken to engage in such a game. You are dangerous. You are full of terrible wrath.

Your touch alone is enough to poison a man. You are dangerously contagious. Many people will die in most dreadful pain because of you, and many will be driven mad. You are fearfully strong. You are destructive. Your veins flow with power. You could be dropped like a nuclear bomb from an airplane, and you would destroy a whole city, a whole state, the entire planet."

The young teacher was utterly astounded. She begged him with humble eyes to be rougher, more brutal and more cynical. When he did as she desired, she openly asked him to be vulgar. And when he had complied with this wish as well, she pressed her leg hard against his and told him that she desperately wanted to meet him in the school yard behind the rubbish bins. He advised her not to do anything rash and to have some consideration toward his future fiancée. L.M. now turned to Katerina, who was sitting on his right, and began stroking her hand in a display of tenderness.

The main course was about to be served. When her food came, Katerina carefully brought each bite to her mouth and chewed with great restraint. It was clear that she felt embarrassed when eating in the presence of others. She could not give herself up to the pleasures of eating. Her mouth was dry, and she swallowed each bite with great effort.

L.M.'s attention was riveted upon a fatty piece of meat on her plate. He watched it like a hawk. As she raised it toward her lips, he jogged her elbow. The fatty piece of meat fell first onto her chin and then tumbled into her lap, leaving a greasy stain on her white dress.

She stiffened, turned pale. One woman shrieked. Another leapt up to help her. The chemistry teacher also sprang to his feet. "It's nothing," he said. "Nothing." He offered to take her to the chemistry lab and remove the greasy stain with chemicals. Katerina grinned apologetically, as though the accident had been her fault.

The young geography mistress asked L.M. to make a

show of being shocked by his fiancée. L.M. complied with her wish. The chemistry teacher took Katerina away and returned with her shortly afterwards. As he returned, he was roaring with laughter, and he told L.M. that he was bringing him Katerina clean all over.

"I don't believe we have met," said L.M. "May I have the honor of introducing myself. I am the director of a coffin manufacturing concern. I shall be counting on you as a client. You will, of course, have the very best."

The chemistry teacher took this as a joke. He laughed. No one else laughed. "Why are you all so silent?" he asked.

"Come on—let's eat! Let's drink! Let's sing!"

His head was huge, red, and squarish. Hairs grew out of his ears and nostrils. His nose and mouth were moist. He took off his jacket. "I'm hot," he said. He began rolling up his shirt sleeves. Two hairy arms emerged. "I can't resist brains," he said.

He first drank a glass of wine and then, setting the glass carefully on the table, set to work on the sheep's head, beginning with the eyes. He skewered one eye on his fork, opened his mouth, and bent down for the bite. A loud scrunching was heard and the fork reappeared, bare.

He then made short work of the other eye. The roast sheep's head now had two dark cavities where the eyes had been. He licked his lips and grunted with satisfaction. He wiped his hands on a napkin and took another gulp of wine.

All eyes were riveted upon him. Everybody watched his movements and waited anxiously for him to attack the brain. He set about it with a will, cracking open the skull with both hands and extricating the brain with two twists of the fork. The brain slithered off his plate and nearly fell to the floor, but he held his hand out just in time to catch it and flip it deftly back onto his plate. In his mouth it was crushed to pulp in a moment. After his feat of juggling he could not help opening his mouth to give a victorious laugh. The brain glistened white in the cavern of his mouth.

L.M. fled to the balcony. Katerina hurried out after him.

L.M. was crying. "What's the matter with you, what's the matter?" she asked.

"Lichten! Lichten!"

"No! He's only our chemistry teacher. He's a good man."

"Lichten! Lichten!"

"Calm yourself! It's all right."

"He killed children! One every day! He had a table arranged for them so that their blood would pour down and fill a glass, then another glass, and another, and another. Four glasses. Corporal Henrich also tried to do it, but he wasn't able." L.M. wept.

Katerina wrung her hands in despair. "Enough, enough!"

"What d'you mean, enough? What d'you mean? Yesterday they ran over a child with a car. An eldest son. They left his mother to wash and dress him by herself. The only help she had was from a hospital nurse who poured hot water over him from a teapot. The mother asked her to cool the water but she said it would make no difference." L.M. sobbed.

Katerina continued to wring her hands. She longed to hold him close and to kiss him many, many times. "Ah, ah," he said. "I've had enough of lying, enough. These lies of mine have led me to the brink of ruin. Enough. I'm through with lying now. I'm telling you the truth: I am prepared to take upon myself responsibility for all human evil and to bear all punishments, to bear all the tribulations and terrors which were ever meant for mankind from beginning to end, and all the pains of all deaths. I am telling you the truth. These are not vain words. I am ready." After this outburst he calmed down.

But now it was Katerina's turn to cry. She wanted in some way to satisfy his wishes, to help him, but she did not know how. "Something is tormenting you," she told him. "What is it? Tell me. Trust in me. I feel as if you are my own. I will do everything I possibly can for you."

L.M. now started crying. He looked deeply into Katerina's eyes. "What can you do for me?" he asked. "You are a child.

You will be sadly deceived. You will be treated like dirt. You will be killed, and your blood will be drunk."

"I am prepared for the sacrifice," she said. "I only want to help you. I have a boundless belief in my ability to help you."

"No," he answered. "No. No, you cannot. I have many enemies. I am surrounded by cunning people. People who wear many masks."

The chemistry teacher suddenly appeared on the balcony. "Aha! Aha!" he said. "So you're here, are you?"

"Yes we are," said L.M. "So what?"

"Oh, nothing, nothing."

"You surely don't think we're still living under the Gestapo and that we can't go where we please."

"Not at all! Far from it!"

"We are what we are, and we are where we wish to be."

"Naturally, naturally!"

The chemistry teacher went away. "He's fallen in love with you."

"No!"

"And you've fallen in love with him."

"No!"

"Yes!"

Katerina became frightened. She warned him: "You mustn't do it."

He took no notice of her warning. "He is obviously courting you. He's constantly appearing naked before you and taking advantage of your longing for hairy, dirty, sticky bodies."

"Oh, please don't. Spare me."

L.M. was merciless. "You have prostituted your soul, Katerina. It is only a short step from immodesty of this sort to debauchery." Katerina stared in astonishment. "Why are you surprised?" asked L.M. "That's how it is. Before long I'll be seeing you tarted up with all the tricks of the trade."

Katerina could not tear her eyes away from him. Her tears welled up. L.M. sneered mockingly: "Now you're crying, but tomorrow you'll be hard at it, fouling your body." Her tears fell unchecked.

"All right, that's enough for now. Pull yourself together. Let's go and hear what they're singing inside." L.M. paused to listen to the song which was drifting out from the main room. "Oho, that's your chemist singing. He's singing a love song. He's singing for you. That songbird of yours is tempting you into his love-nest with music. And what do you think? Do you really think I'm going to allow you to make a cuckold of me? Do you think I'm so naive as not to have guessed that he had his fingers on your pretty body while he was removing the stain from your dress?"

Katerina was choking with tears. "How ravishing it must have been to yield your charms to those rough, hairy paws. You're a great one for crying. Enough of these female lies. Enough of these female crocodile tears. I don't fall for such things. I can see through women. Women have brought down a million evils on men. They have trampled us underfoot. Even their slightest gesture, designed for seduction, stirs up a thousand evils. Their short, tight dresses are the cause of a million. They enjoy the privilege of being the weaker sex. And that is the greatest lie in the world. It is their basic aim to make fools of men. Get out of my sight. I cannot bear to see your hypocritical tears.

"O-ho, oo-ho, ho." L.M. was trying out his voice. "Ah-haa, a-ha, ha. Go back where you came from, go back. You cannot save me. You cannot even save yourself. Uh-hu, uu-u-hu, uha." His vocal chords were remarkably well strung.

He began to sing. He sang a ballad about a forty-year-old woman lamenting the young man who had left her: "He has gone, ah, my strong young man has gone—he who knew how to lure me into love on the floorboards of a rented room, ah, he is gone, ah, my young man!" He left a deep impression upon the loveliest woman present, both by the passion of his voice and by the short, meaningful looks he frequently cast her. She gazed down at him with a gentle smile. She seemed to be looking from above, almost protectively. This was because she was conscious of her stunning beauty, her superior social position (the Director treated her husband with the greatest friendliness), her noble appearance, which was accentuated by the fine proportions of her well-shaped body, and, finally, because she carried her forty years with grace.

L.M. took advantage of a moment when her husband was looking through an album with the Director and, after first asking her husband's permission, invited her to dance. She readily agreed. As they danced she became more and more solicitous. A tango was being played.

L.M. decided to rely only on the power of words. "You think I'm crazy," he told her. "I am a man of free will, and that alone is quite sufficient for people to consider me mad. The great innovators in history have always been considered mad in the eyes of their contemporaries. So, I might apply a special method to you, one which is tried and tested —I might pay court to you in a way guaranteed to bring one hundred per cent success. I might fire you with the spark of revolt and set your apparently calm and peaceful being alight with the most violent flame. I might become the wizard of your body. In no time at all I could succeed in making you rip off your false and hypocritical mask of dignity and force you to display your vulgar charms openly for sale. This is what you are waiting for—this moment, this salvation, a savior for your body. But I won't use that method. You do not deserve to sink so low. I shall simply take up the role of a businessman offering a client his services: professional love of the highest quality, utmost discretion guaranteed. Wait for me. I shall come."

The second part of the dance now followed. They did not speak. The onus was on her to tell him whatever she wished, to make use of his madness as an excuse. But although the whole question of madness had been broached and discussed thoroughly, she said nothing. She remained silent. He nevertheless decided to make a discreet attempt to establish some kind of communication through bodily contact. But, as was to be expected, she rejected his advances.

L.M. interpreted this reaction, together with her frowning anger and her show of being offended, as an indication of the onset of bodily revolt. He escorted her politely back to her place and thanked her. He also thanked her husband.

"Dance with me, L.M.," said the young geography mistress.

"I must find a hawker for you," he answered. "You'd make an attractive barter." She went out of her way to flash him an enchanting smile, to impress him with the fact that she had understood what he had said and that she was flattered by it, but for the sake of politeness she had turned it into a joke.

L.M. considered that she had no moral right to hide behind a facade of politeness. He decided to tell her what he thought. "You're garbage. You can wait for me behind the rubbish bins only under one condition—that you stand on one leg for ten minutes, holding the tip of your nose between your thumb and index finger." She gave him a savage look, which threatened to make him pay dearly for his insolence and for taking unfair advantage of her weakness toward him. But it was clear to L.M. that she was pretending, that his impudence was by no means distasteful to her.

As she went out toward the door to carry out her assigned task, L.M. crossed over to Katerina and said to her, "The presence of that cave man in our midst causes me great suffering and distress. All my pleasure is clouded over, and all the more so because I caught you stealing a look at his hands. And so, for the reason just mentioned, and because of your excessive corpulence, I find I am unable to ask you for the pleasure of a dance."

The young geography mistress explained her curious posture to the people around her by saying that she had agreed to stand like that on a bet. They all laughed at the joke. The headmaster made endless efforts to find out just what kind of bet it was and with whom it had been made. She refused to answer. She did her very best to pass the whole matter off as a piece of fun.

"The ten minutes are up," said L.M. She removed her fingers from the tip of her nose and stood on both feet. Some people applauded. She did not know what to do. She began to laugh, hoping to join in the general mood of merriment and so to leave the impression that the whole affair was really no more than a bet made in fun.

The headmaster looked at her with suspicion. With irony he once more reverted to the bet. "I've nothing against the young lady's proving herself to you," said L.M. The young geography mistress shook her head and made an effort to laugh it off.

The music began again, another dance. The young teacher beseeched L.M. to invite her to dance and so to release her from the curious gaze of the onlookers. L.M. did not particularly like the dance.

Suddenly, however, a wave of enthusiasm swept over him. He felt like shouting for joy. He executed some remarkable steps involving double leg movements, to the great delight of the people watching. They formed a circle around him and clapped in time to the beat.

"Behind the rubbish bins, behind the rubbish bins," the young geography mistress repeated several times.

"Is your mother still alive?" L.M. shouted loudly.

"No."

"It is her blessed fortune to be dead; you will give birth to the Anti-Christ." At a suitable moment she left.

L.M. raised his hand as a sign that he wished to speak. "People are united by the triumphant power of love," he began. "It is the triumphant power of love which makes them good, beautiful, and free. Love. It generates all life. What is left to us in this ruined world, trembling on the brink of a dreadful war, except to turn to love for our salvation, to bear witness to the power of its divinity, to erect temples and statues, to make idols, and to offer ourselves to love as true believers. For, in the end, what is the purpose of my existence and of your existence, if we have no one to love? It is only through those whom we love that we justify our existence and take shelter under the protection of the laws by which we were created. We are the fruit of love, and we, ourselves, must bear new fruit." He scanned his audience with a glance, then continued: "And now, by way of exemplifying what I have been saying, allow me to announce my engagement."

Everybody recoiled slightly and shot questioning glances at him. With the gesture of a martyr he pointed toward Katerina.

Katerina blushed in confusion. He crossed to her and formally offered her his hand. She stood up. She made a movement with her hand as if to hide a greasy stain on her lap, but then she realized that this would be even more ridiculous, and so she gave up the attempt. "Let's have a tango please, a tango," said L.M.

Katerina was considerably larger than L.M. She broke out in a sweat of embarrassment. She could hardly move her legs, and she danced heavily, clumsily, often out of time with the music.

Silence fell. There were pitying looks on all faces. The headmaster glanced severely at L.M. He was convinced that L.M. wanted to marry Katerina because of her money.

L.B. broke off the dance and looked questioningly at everybody. He saved his last glance for the doctor. "I've had my eye on you the whole time," he said. "You want to call in the officers of the law and have me arrested. You consider me an imposter, a confidence man playing on people's naivete. You are wrong. You are no match for me. I am so sensitive and highly strung that I can describe infallibly what each person is thinking, whether his thoughts are benign or malign. My senses have grown sharp. My soul is sensitive, and I am highly strung.

"Let's get this straight. If we want to make any progress

we must first come to terms with the hypocrites. What I mean is that if you have anything to tell me you must first tear the mask from your face. And you want to tell me that I announced my engagement to this woman only because I want to get my hands on her savings. First rip off your mask, then tell me that.

"Ah, what have we come to?" L.M. now turned to the crowd as though he were addressing a meeting. "What have we come to? We cannot go on allowing the Napoleon Bonapartes among us to cut our cloth to suit their tastes. How long are we going to put up with these people who say one thing and do another? It is not the politicians who should make the decisions nowadays; it's the people themselves who must decide. And if we don't, we'll be ruined."

The headmaster smiled. In his opinion L.M. was a man likely to indulge in mad excesses, a man from whom anything might be expected. "You think I'm a madman?" asked L.M. "Or, to put it more precisely, you don't really think I'm mad, but that's how you'd like to pass me off. It's an old, well-tried method which the authorities always resort to for getting rid of ideas. Don't try it, I warn you. I know these tricks. Many things are known to me. I know the schemes you're plotting in that big bald head of yours. I'm very well informed about world affairs. Try telling somebody else about your great love of freedom and peace. Try telling somebody else about the homage you pay to those who fell in the cause of freedom. You only know how many people fell, and you use those numbers in your calculations. It gives you a great kick to hear these teachers applauding your slick words. You speak with feigned enthusiasm about the dress of some actress. Stupidity is more dreadful than war. What sort of peace is this, in which great minds are exposed to ridicule? One cannot possibly mention ideals in the same breath as a woman's dress, and yet that is just what these teachers were doing today in the classroom in order to try to curry favor with the children. How will they be able to gaze into the clear lakes of the children's eyes, how will they dare to enter the classroom with such unclean hearts?"

The headmaster was still grinning blandly, hoping to smile his way out of an awkward situation. "You are laughing again," said L.M. "Don't, I warn you. You are an old fox, but I am an angry wolf. Maybe I do not understand cunning, but I understand force. I have constantly before me the image of myself brandishing a hammer at an enormous ingot of steel. Millions of sparks leap out into space. So, I'm warning you, don't get high and mighty with me. Money plays absolutely no part in my emotional life. Therein lies my strength. And so, I am warning you not only of your mistakes but also of my power. When I return I shall be implacable but just." L.M. took Katerina's arm and they departed together.

L.M. glanced round him. The others were in the school yard. At the far end he spotted the rubbish bin and beside it the silhouette of the young geography mistress who was signaling desperately to him with her hand. L.M. laughed and, drawing Katerina after him, went out into the street. A heart-rending cry reached them from the yard. L.M. doubled up with laughter. They walked on, L.M. in front, Katerina following.

They left the confines of the city. A ponderous silence and a heavy oppressiveness made them shudder. L.M. looked up at the sky. It was as clear as it had been for the past two months. At first sight all seemed well, yet L.M. felt as if he were being stalked by something hidden and menacing. He examined the edges of the sky and saw that they were clear and dry. But when he lowered his eyes, he had the impression that heavy shadows were lurking beneath the horizon.

L.M. and Katerina continued on their way. It was difficult to cut a passage through the air. They were perspiring profusely. Her sweat stank. She could hardly walk. She tired quickly because of her weight. Her breathing was painful. Her dress got caught on a wire. She stood and sighed heav-

ily. L.M. slapped her savagely across the cheek, and she
fell without a sound at his feet.

IV

"Now we're in a trap," thought L.M. "Somebody must
have given us away. How, otherwise, could this have happened? First, there must have been shadows creeping close
to the ground, then low clouds must have filled the sky.
They must have been like buffaloes, those clouds. The moon
was squeezed tight, fighting for breath, and the tops of the
trees were shaking with fear. But nobody saw any of this.
Now the clouds are pressing down upon us. They are so
close I feel I could touch them by raising my hand. It is silent
and very dark. One can hardly see anything."

Katerina was lying beside him. Her skin was unusually
white. She did not want to cover herself. She felt no shame.
Nothing made any difference to her; she only wanted to lie
there. L.M. plucked up his courage and broke the stillness
with a sudden movement.

He was searching on the ground for some piece of her
scattered clothing. Whenever he found a garment, he flung
it at her eyes, which were now fixed upon him, unnaturally
wide and staring. She was motionless.

A piece of her underclothing was now draped across her
eyes. L.M. straightened up. A fierce pain shot through his
spine. He took a first step and bent over double.

"No," she said, almost inaudibly. "No."

He was terrified, trembling. "I have a most pressing need,"
he said. "Back in a second. Be so good as to let me go."

She did not answer. Her eyes could not be seen.

He bent over as close as possible to the ground and
walked with great care. Then he stopped and looked back.
Behind him he could make out the contours of Katerina's
huge, white body. L.M. straightened up and fled, as fast as
his legs would carry him.

His legs felt heavy, but he forced them to move. His

footsteps fell undirected on the dusty road and echoed dully in the night silence. He found the going hard. His heart throbbed painfully.

He had the impression that he was gaining no ground. He was hemmed in on all sides and could hardly breathe. He flung his head desperately left and right, to make breathing easier. The air he sucked in was warm and thick. It scorched his lungs. Salt sweat ran into his eyes and mouth. After he had stopped running, the sweat continued to break out on his neck and chest and to trickle over his back and down his legs.

He was wearing with his yellow cotton jacket a white shirt and a red tie. His feet were slipping, as if his shoes were full of mud. He could hardly drag himself along the dusty road. Thick dust stopped his nose and stuck to his face. He held his hands out in front of him to force a passage through the air. He tried to avoid stumbling over hard objects.

He tried to think of something, but his mind was exhausted. All the same he forced himself to concentrate so that he might at least escape from this silence and find his way to the road leading into town. He was now walking more easily. He no longer felt the thick layer of dust underfoot. The ground had become firmer.

He continued like this for some time, not knowing his direction and forcing his way through the air with his hands. Then all of a sudden he noticed ahead of him, weakly illuminated, the trunk of a tree and its upper branches. He looked beyond it and tried to discover the source of the light, and he saw, not far away, the city.

He was constricted by the clouds, choked, weary. L.M. looked around to see if he could recognize his surroundings. In front of him he could make out a dark field with bushes and poplars, behind him a dark building with a tall chimney, to his right an orchard, and to his left, right next to him, the whitish sheen of the road.

L.M. stood on the same spot for quite some time; he was incapable of attempting anything. His thoughts were ponderous, sticky, his head heavy, fuddled, watery. Saliva trickled from his mouth. Sweat was oozing out of every pore and running down to his fingertips. His heart was beating painfully and dully. At last his legs, of their own accord, set out for the lights of the city.

He walked for a long time, struggling to keep his bearings. Suddenly he came to a slope. It might have been a dike. His legs simply stopped in front of the rise.

There was no more strength or courage left in them. Nothing could force them to make the effort required to overcome this obstacle. A long time passed. He stayed where he was, in front of the dike, and began to think. Finally he managed to realize that it would be better if he bent down and tried to climb the slope on his hands and knees.

Moving on all fours, dragging himself along on his stomach, his elbows, and his knees, he struggled to the top of the rise. Utterly exhausted, he collapsed on the hard ground. Fierce waves of heat now began to roll over him. The clouds were hovering above him. Salt water was oozing from every pore, so hot that it seemed to scald him. The beating of his heart shook his whole body. He sighed and groaned with pain; this relieved him slightly. The more inarticulate his groaning became, the greater was his relief.

Finally the bursts of boiling heat subsided, and he calmed himself. He could now see the city close at hand. He was almost there. He needed only to walk downhill and enter the first suburban street to find himself on the edge of the town.

He longed desperately to drag himself as far as his flat. He wanted to be brave and to overcome this last obstacle of distance. He gritted his teeth and slowly raised his body from the ground. His collarbone grated ominously. He straightened up and hovered indecisively at the top of the slope.

He forced himself to take a step. He took two steps, but

his legs, anticipating the effort that lay ahead, lost their strength and, overcome with cowardice, began to tremble. He teetered and then immediately fell to his knees.

He remained for some time like this. Then the thought occurred to him that he must look like an old man. "How old am I?" he wondered. He searched his memories for a long time, rearranging them to bring all his attention to bear on the problem, but he could not remember. He searched back through the past and tried to track down a particular moment which might help him to calculate his age correctly, but he had no success. He felt inclined to reject all rational processes, but in the end he overcame this desire and continued his tireless search into the past.

This persistence would, he hoped, serve to buoy up his foundering consciousness. But his disconnected thoughts slipped away from him; he was unable to stay them. Quite out of the blue it suddenly struck him that he had also forgotten his name. He wondered what he was doing in this place and where he was headed. He found no answer. Then, without knowing how or from where the strength came to him, he rose to his feet again and stood upright at the top of the slope.

Before his legs had the chance to go on strike and let him down a second time, he forced them to run downhill. But his legs, after making the first few large steps out of sheer inertia, no longer felt the ground beneath them and folded as if they had been scythed from under him. L.M. fell on his face. His face landed in something soft and smelly. He was utterly exhausted.

He did not know how long he lay like this. He was not conscious of the passage of time. Much later he felt that something of great importance was happening around him. Sounds came to him. Splashing, crackling, and a sound like sighing. He became conscious of something beating him gently over his head, neck, and back. A strong shiver coursed through his body. He smelt the sharp smell of the

earth. Finally he realized that a warm rain was falling
from the sky.

A heavy sigh escaped from his throat. He began to breathe
easily and rhythmically. He felt a pleasant sense of relax-
ation and of strength returning to his body. He stretched
out with deep pleasure and then turned over on his back.
The rain was falling gently and quietly. Then it became
heavier and heavier. It had a miraculous effect on his ex-
tended body. He kept his eyes closed. It was pleasant to
have the rain washing his face.

Time passed slowly, and he again felt active, strong, and
clean. He soon would be able to stand up and set off toward home with firm steps. But he postponed this until
later. He could not so easily abandon his comfortable position. He settled into an even more comfortable position and,
spreading out his arms and legs, surrendered himself completely to the gentle rain.

Epilogue

It turned out that his flat had not been far away. It was
stifling hot in his room. L.M. quickly opened the windows,
then he changed his clothes. The dry clothes cooled him.

He looked at the clock: five fifteen. He picked up the
rope with the noose at the end and, as usual, aimed thirty
throws at the door handle. One throw for each year of his
life. This time he did not succeed once in hooking the
handle.

He glanced at the clock again: five twenty-five. He stood
by the window, holding the noose. He looked out at the sky.
Dawn was brightening in the east. The sky was suffused
with silver light. The clouds began to break up and to scatter in different directions.

Suddenly the sun appeared; its rays were brisk, fresh
and cheerful. L.M. gazed at the city spread out below him.
It was clean and shimmering. The walls of the houses were

damp. The roofs glittered as if they had been brushed with gold.

Sounds of life stirred around him; movements caught his eye. The shutters were being rolled up on the neighboring buildings. Windows were flung open. People stretched their sleepy limbs. He could hear the sound of wooden clogs in the corridors. Powerful jets of water spurted from the taps.

The milkman appeared below in the park. The young mother, with an apron around her waist, came down quickly to collect her milk. Her younger son, who had obviously not slept long enough, came out onto the balcony in his pajamas, crying. A yellow bumblebee buzzed playfully past L.M.'s nose on its way down toward the green park.

Somewhere in the city a clock was striking the hour. At last the cheerful little office girl appeared on the balcony. There was something fresh and vital in her appearance. She laughed gaily and then, with a wave of her hand, ran back inside.

She'll be downstairs in a minute, L.M. thought to himself. I'll not be able to find a better moment. Now I'll give her something to laugh about. She'll carry me in her thoughts all her life. In about sixty seconds she ought to appear below.

L.M. swiftly tied the rope to the side of the window and made all the other preparations necessary for hanging himself. Then he hanged himself. When the cheerful office girl came out of the downstairs door and looked up at his window to show that she was still eager to play the game, he was already swinging at the end of the rope. His game was over.